English Language Skills

Level One

My name is _____.

I come from _____.

My English class is in room _____.

Published by
Boyer Educational Resources
for worldwide distribution.

Phone/fax +61 2 4739 1538
Web address: www.boyereducation.com.au

Acknowledgments

I would like to express my thanks to the following people for their contribution to the final presentation of this book:

Firstly, I would like to thank the teachers who trialed material in this book and suggested improvements. In particular, I wish to thank Kim Alexander, Marie Maguire and Maria Muronie for their time and constructive feedback regarding the material included in the book. Also, I would like to thank Maria Reed and Dianne Bernoth for their feedback on the general content and layout of the book. I would like to thank Jeanette Christian for her proofreading and editing skills. I am very appreciative to Jim Astley for his quality audio recording, editing and advice given during the production of the audio CD which accompanies this resource. Thank you also to Len Boyer, Jeanette Christian and Ben Astley for lending their voices for the sound recordings.

Also, I want to thank my dear husband, Len, for his encouragement and support throughout the project. And finally, as always I am indebted to the many students who have given me the necessary insight into the language needs of English language learners around the world.

The following images used herein were obtained from IMSI's MasterClips Collection, 1895 Francisco Blvd. East, San Rafael, CA 94901-5506, USA: page 44, 80 (1). Clip art images on page 10, 2 2 (1, 2, 5) 40 (9), 53 (b, c, f), 56 (1, 2, 4, 7) 57, 66, 70, 78, 79, 80, 81 were obtained from Microsoft's clip Gallery, Microsoft Pty Ltd. Images on page 39 (a, b, e, f, g), 40 (2, 3, 5, 6, 7) were obtained from Greenstreet Collections. Illustrations on pages 15 (bottom), 27 (5 & 13) 29, 30 (6), 58, 59 (e) are by Matthew J Larwood. Other illustrations are by Susan Boyer. Cover images were obtained from istockphoto.com

Boyer, Susan
English Language Skills – Level One Student's Workbook
ISBN 978 1 877074 29 5

Copyright laws allow for a maximum of one chapter or 10% of this book, whichever is the greater, to be copied by educational institutions for educational purposes provided that the educational institution has given a remuneration notice to the copyright agency of the relevant country. For example, enquiries within Australia should be directed to Copyright Agency Limited (CAL) Information can be found at www.copyright.com.au or email info@copyright.com.au.

For enquiries in the United Kingdom, information can be obtained from www.alcs.co.uk.

Enquiries for copying for any other purpose should be made to the publisher at the address below.

No part of this publication may be reproduced, stored in a retrieval system or transmitted in any form or by any means electronic, mechanical, photocopying, recording or otherwise, without the prior consent of the publisher.

© Boyer Educational Resources 2009,

[7th] Print, 2012

© Boyer Educational Resources: Phone/fax +61 2 4739 1538
   e-mail: boyer@eftel.net.au
   www.boyereducation.com.au
   www.englishebooks.com.au (for download of eBook & eAudio versions of our resources)

English Language Skills - Level 1 Contents

Numbers and words	Page 1
English alphabet letters; Spelling aloud - English letters and words	2-3

Unit 1 - English Class   4

- Listening for information
- Ken's English class - Capital letters
- Writing information on a form
- Things in the classroom
- My English class
- Saying English words – syllables
- Counting things
- Signs
- Greeting and saying goodbye
- Asking for directions

Unit 2 – Talking about People   18

- Family words
- Giving information about me
- Rona Green – A form - Name and address
- Giving information about other people
- Describing people – clothes
- Talking about other people – photographs
- Asking questions
- Using pronouns
- Saying English words – syllables
- Giving information – using verbs

Unit 3 – Everyday Activities   34

- Can you swim?
- What can John and Kate do?
- Talking about activities we like doing
- What do you like doing?
- Jobs - What do people do in their jobs?
- Stories about other people
- Writing about other people

Unit 4 – Talking about Time and Events   44

- Months of the year
- What is the date? What is the time?
- Talking about routine - Boris and Natasha's routine
- How often?
- Past, present and future time
- Asking questions about the past
- Giving information about the past
- Mai's weekend
- Jo's story
- Past tense verbs
- Special days
- Bob's story - Bella's story - Our holiday

English Language Skills - Level 1 Contents

Unit 5 – Health and Safety   Page 60

     Parts of the body.
     Symptoms.
     Medical checkups
     Saying you don't understand
     Reading medicine labels
     At the pharmacy or chemist
     Staying healthy.
     Emergency service - Emergency calls.

Unit 6 – Shopping and Services   70

     How many?
     Asking for things
     Offering food and drinks
     Shopping in the supermarket
     Asking where
     Groceries – How many? A shopping list
     What is in the fridge?
     Garage sale; How much?
     Buying lunch
     Matilda's story

Unit 7 – Going Places   80

     Places in the town and city
     Adam's story
     Buying a train ticket – Read the train timetable
     Adam's suburb - Reading a map
     This year
     Next year

Answers   88 - 100

Teacher's Note: For a more detailed overview of the unit contents of this book,
       see **English Language Skills - Level 1 Teacher's Book**.

The symbol means **listen** to the track on the audio CD.

The symbol means **practise speaking** with another person.

The symbol means **write** words.

The symbol means there is a related activity in the Teacher's Book

Complementary support material for the topics, lessons and exercises in this book can be found in *'Word Building Activities for Beginners of English'* (Boyer Educational Resources, 2009). See back cover for details.

Numbers and words

 Listen. Read and say the names of the numbers.

1 one	2 two	3 three	4 four	5 five
6 six	7 seven	8 eight	9 nine	10 ten
11 eleven	12 twelve	13 thirteen	14 fourteen	15 fifteen
16 sixteen	17 seventeen	18 eighteen	19 nineteen	20 twenty

Using numbers

We use numbers to count 'how many' people or things. How many people are in your classroom? _____

How many chairs are in your classroom? _____

We use numbers to give information. What is the phone number where you learn English? _____

English Language Skills - Level 1

English alphabet letters

There are 26 **letters** used to write English words.

Listen and **say** the name of each letter.

a b c d e f g h i j k l m n o p q r s t u v w x y z

Listen again and **write** the letters.

a _

The letters **a e i o u** are **vowel** letters. Highlight the five vowel letters.

Your teacher will say the names of letters. Mark the letters you hear with a tick.

a	b	c	d	e	f	g	h	i	j	k	l	m
n	o	p	q	r	s	t	u	v	w	x	y	z

Teacher's Note: See more activities in the Teacher's Book.

Spelling aloud – English letters and words

Listen. (Track 4)

a for apples 	b for beetle 	c for cat 	d for dog 	e for eggs 	f for father 	g for glasses 
h for hat 	i for insects 	j for jacket 	k for kangaroo 	l for letter 	m for money 	n for  no
o for oranges 	p for people 	q  for queue	r for rabbit 	s for sun 	t for tea 	u for umbrella 
	v for vegetables 	w for woman 	x for x-ray 	y for  yes	z for zoo 	

✏ Highlight the five vowel letters.

Names of people begin with a capital letter:

A B C D E F G H I J K L M N O P Q R S T U V W X Y Z

🐭 Write you name. _____  Spell your name to another person.

English Language Skills – Level 1   3   © Boyer Educational Resources

Names of people and countries begin with a capital letter.

A B C D E F G H I J K L M N O P Q R S T U V W X Y Z

✎ Write the names of people and places from page 4.

Names of people	Names of places

✎ Write: My name is _____

I come from _____

Where is your country?

✎ Write the sentences correctly.

1. My Kim name is. _____

2. come from China I. _____

Listening for information

Track 6 🎧 Listen to the first names and countries of three people.
Listen for the spelling.

Write the names: Write the countries:

1. _____   1. _____

2. _____   2. _____

3. _____   3. _____

Track 7 🎧 Listen and write the name and the address.
Listen for the spelling.

Can I have your full name and address please.

¹ Yes. My first name is _ _ _.
² My surname is _ _ _ _ _ _ _.
³ My address is 221 _ _ _ _ _ Street.
⁴ My suburb is _ _ _ _ _ _ _ _ _.
⁵ My postcode is _ _ _ _

 Write the information on the form.

1. First name:	2. Surname:
3. Address: _____	
4. Suburb: _____	
5. Postcode: _____	

Always write the <u>first letter as a capital</u> for names of people and places.

English Language Skills - Level 1

Ken's English class

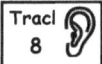 **Listen** to the story about Ken's class.

My name is Ken. I come from China. I go to English class on Monday and Friday to practise reading.
There are fifteen students in my class.
Three people come from China. One person comes from India. Two people come from Vietnam. Three people come from South America. Two people come from Turkey. Two people come from Africa and two people come from Russia.

Write a short story about you and your class.

My name is _____

I come from _____

I go to English class on _____

There are _____ students in my class.

_____

_____

_____

_____

Capital letters

A B C D E F G H I J K L M N O P Q R S T U V W X Y Z

We write a capital letter for the first letter of names
of <u>people</u>, <u>countries</u>, <u>days</u> and <u>languages</u>.

 Highlight 13 writing mistakes in Ken's story below.

My name is ken. I come from china. I go to english class on monday and friday to practise reading. There are fifteen students in my class. Three people come from china. One person comes from india.
Two people come from vietnam. Three people come from south america. Two people come from turkey. Two people come from africa and two people come from russia.

Write the story again correctly.

Write the capital letters

A _ Z

a b c d e f g h i j k l m n o p q r s t u v w x y z

Writing information on a form

 **Listen** and **read** the words.

| 1. first name | 2. surname | 3. address | 4. postcode |
| 5. phone number | 6. date of birth | 7. signature | |

 Write the words

a. *first name* _____ = your name

b. _____ = your family name

c. _____ =

d. _____ =

e. _____ =

f. _____ =

g. _____ =

 Write information about you on the form.

1. First name:	2. Surname:
3. Address:	
4. Postcode:	
5. Phone number:	6. Date of Birth: Date Month Year ___ / ___ / ___
7. Signature:	

English Language Skills - Level 1

Things in the classroom

Track 10 **Listen**

| 1. scissors | 2. pencils | 3. rubber | 4. highlighter | 5. ruler |
| 6. pens | 7. chair and desk | | 8. folder | |

Write

a. _____

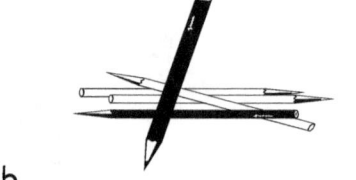

b. _____

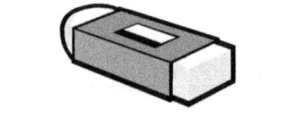

c. _____

d. _____

e. _____

f. _____

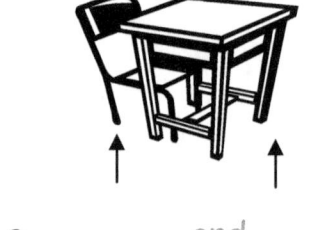

g _____ and _____

i _____

These words are <u>nouns</u>. **Nouns** are the **names** of **things**.

Do **you** have the things you need?

Things I need:	Yes, I have it. ✓	No, I don't have it. ✗
a pen		
a pencil		
a highlighter		
a ruler		
a folder		

Things I need: _____ _____

My English class

Read the names of the days with your teacher.

Monday   Tuesday   Wednesday   Thursday   Friday   Saturday   Sunday

Write the days you come to English class?

_____

What time does your class **start**? _____

What time does your class **finish**? _____

What is your teacher's name? _____

Things in your classroom

What things can you see in your classroom?

Ask your teacher: What is this called in English?
How do you spell it?

Write the names of things in your classroom.

_____   _____

_____   _____

_____   _____

_____   _____   chair   window

Listen and say the words after your teacher.

Saying English words - syllables

We say words by putting sounds together. A group of sounds that go together in a word is called a syllable.

A syllable can be a word or part of a word.

Track 11   1. Listen to the syllables in these words.

One-syllable words	Two-syllable words	Three-syllable words
pen name chair	window ruler English	highlighter Saturday

2. Listen and decide how many syllables in each word.
   Write 1, 2 or 3

door	1	scissors	☐	name	☐	pencil	☐
teacher	☐	desk	☐	surname	☐	telephone	☐
student	☐	classroom	☐	word	☐	sentence	☐
syllable	☐	book	☐	ruler	☐	story	☐

Together with your teacher:

- Look at your list of things in your classroom on page 11.
  Say the words. How many syllables are in each word?

- Find the names of countries in Unit 1.
  Say each country name. How many syllables are in each name?

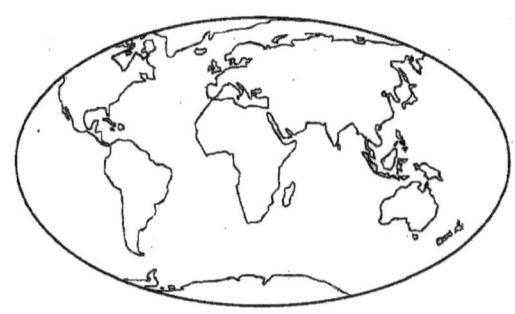

English Language Skills - Level 1   © Boyer Educational Resources

Counting things

When we count two or more things we add 's' to words.

 **Listen**: two student<u>s</u>  four book<u>s</u>

We add '**es**' to some words. The '**es**' can make another syllable.

Listen: one watch  ⟶ two watch<u>**es**</u>

one glass ⟶ two glass<u>**es**</u>

Listen and ⟨circle⟩ the word you hear: **one** thing or **two** things

1. watch ⟨watches⟩
2. book books
3. pencil pencils
4. student students
5. glass glasses

How many?

When we talk about <u>one thing</u>, we say: <u>There is</u> …   **There is** one door.

When we talk about <u>two or more things</u>, we say: <u>There are</u>…

There are two windows.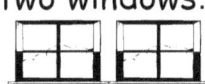

Talk about things in your classroom.

 Write sentences about things in your classroom.

There is one_____

There are _____

_____

English Language Skills - Level 1

Signs

Some signs are written in CAPITAL LETTERS.

Track 13 Listen and read the words on the signs.

1. LIBRARY   2. EXIT   3. CANTEEN   4. NO PARKING

5. ENQUIRIES   6. TOILET

7. LOST PROPERTY   8. NO SMOKING

Write the words next to the pictures.

a. __NO PARKING__ - do **not** park a car here

b. _____ -

c. _____ - a place to buy food

d. _____ - way out

e. _____ -

f. _____ - do **not** smoke here

g. _____ -

h. _____ -

Homework: What other signs can you see?

Write the signs in your book. Ask your teacher: What does this mean?

English Language Skills - Level 1   14   © Boyer Educational Resources

Greeting and saying goodbye

1. Greeting people for the first time

 **Listen** and repeat.   Pleased to meet you.
Hello. It's nice to meet you.

2. Greeting people you know

 **Listen** and repeat.   Hello. How are you?
Hi. How are you going?
Hi. Nice to see you.

3. Saying Goodbye

Listen and repeat.   Well I'd better go now
Bye now.
See you later.
See you.

4. Saying hello and goodbye

 **Listen**.
 Write the words on the lines.

| How | thanks | good | How | go | Bye |

Len: Hello Sue. _____¹ are you?

Sue: Really well_____². How was your weekend?

Len: Really _____³, thank you.

_____⁴ was your weekend?

Sue: It was great.

Len: That's good.

Sue: Well I'd better _____⁵. See you later.

Len: Yes. _____⁶ now.

 Practise the conversation with another person.

Asking for directions

Listen to people asking for directions.

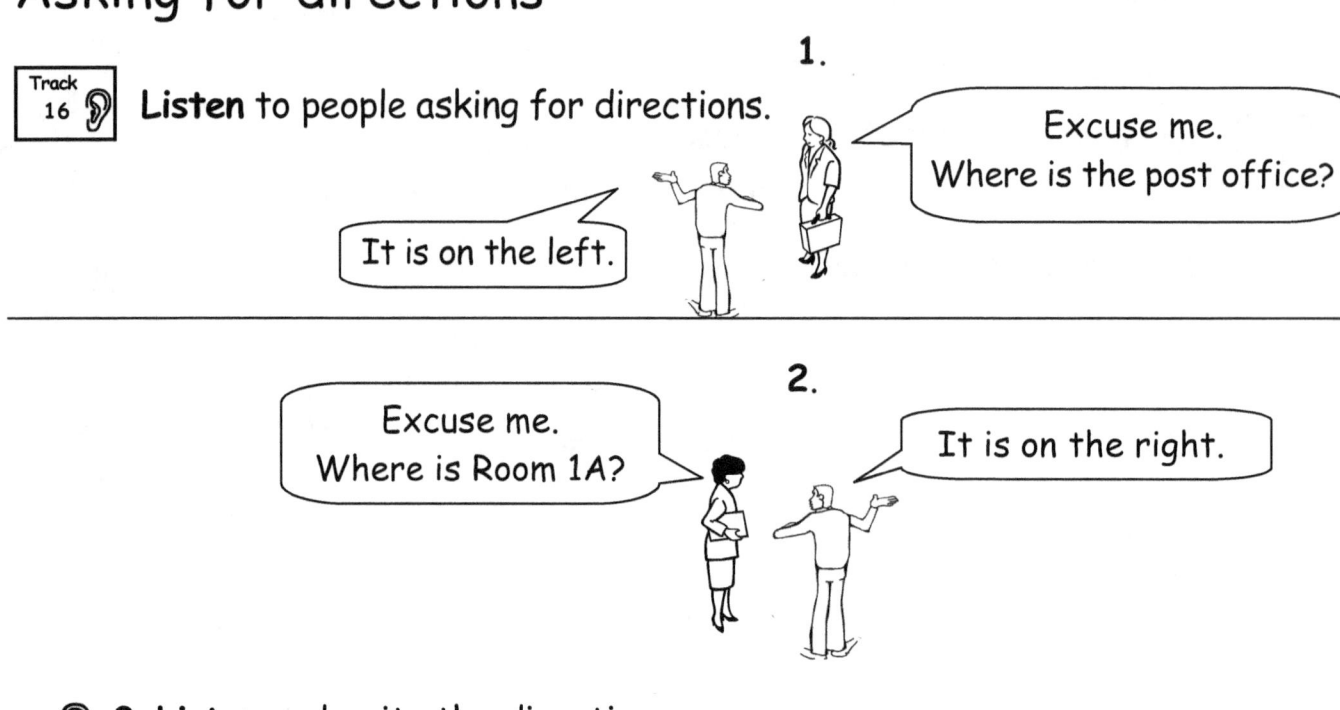

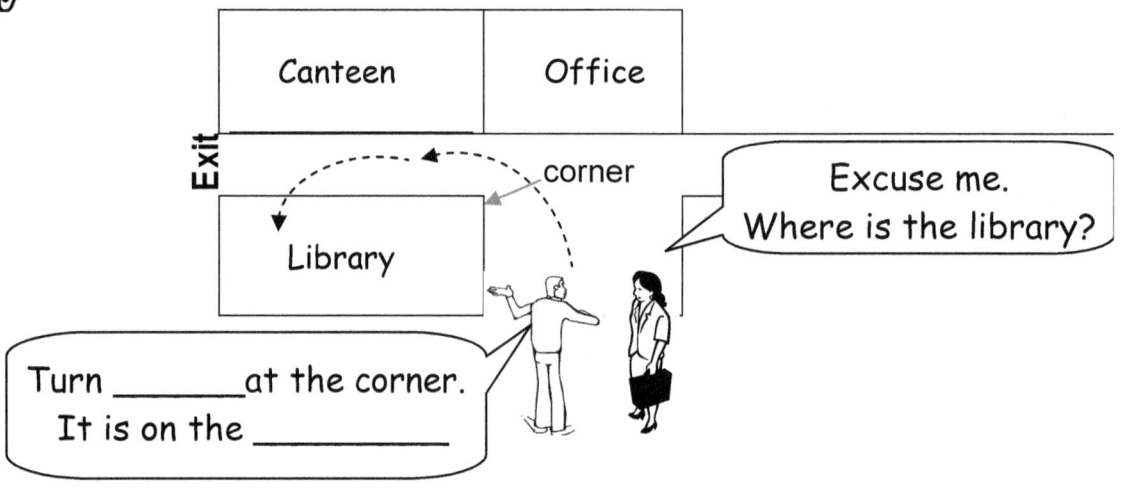

3. Listen and write the direction.

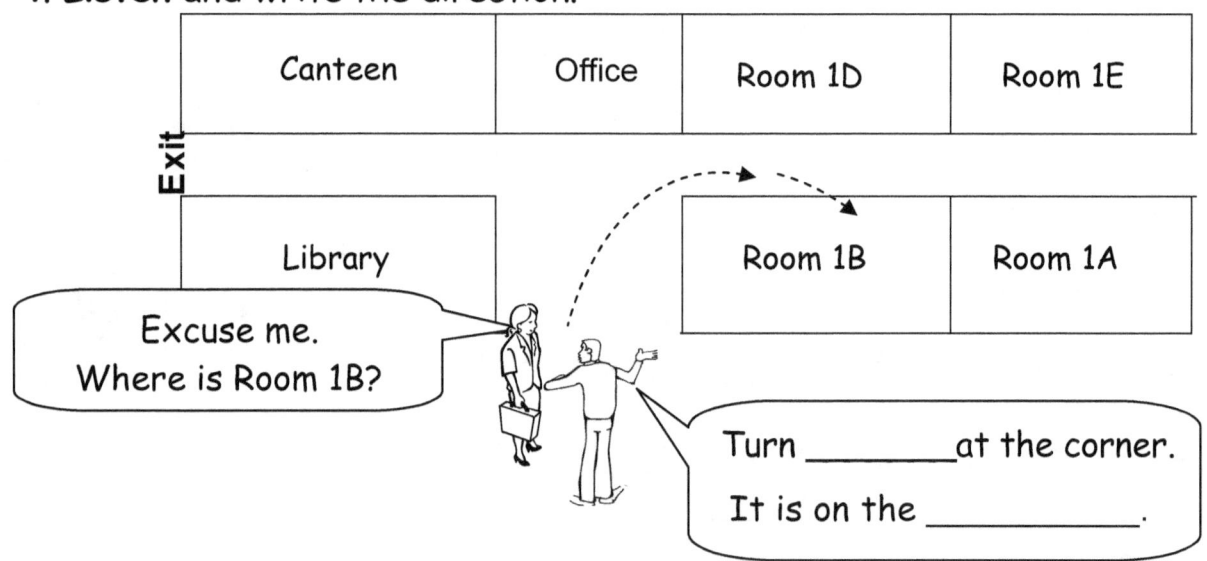

Turn _____ at the corner.
It is on the _____

4. Listen and write the direction.

Turn _____ at the corner.
It is on the _____.

5. Listen and write the direction.

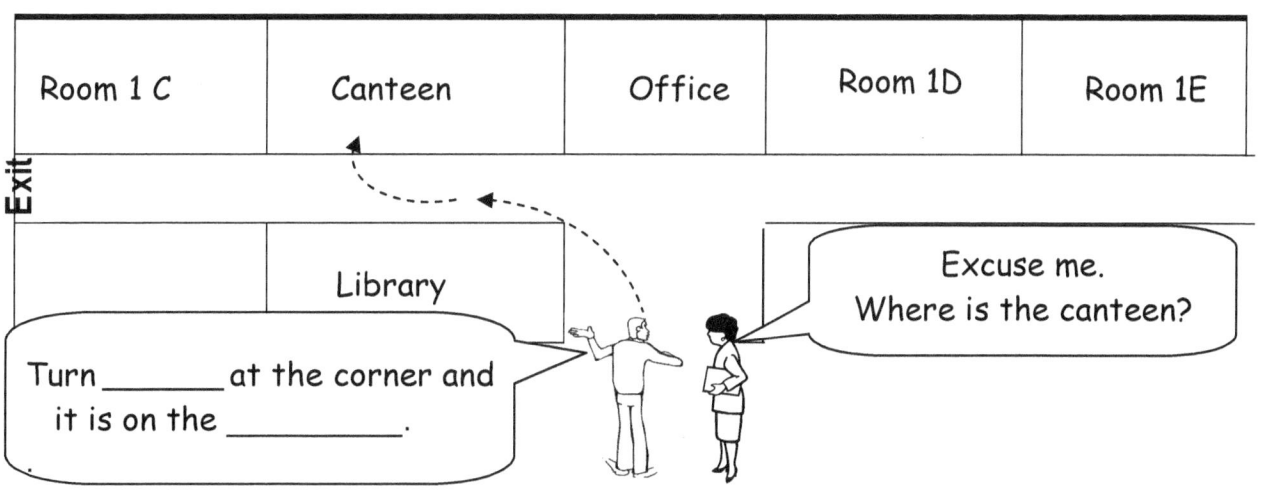

 Practise the conversations.

Words and sounds

 Listen.
One word has a different vowel sound. Circle the different word.

pl<u>ea</u>se   m<u>e</u>   t<u>e</u>n   thr<u>ee</u>   s<u>ee</u>

What can you do now?

Put a tick ☑ next to things you can do.

1. I can write and spell my name and country aloud. ☐
2. I can listen and write information. ☐
3. I can write information on a form. ☐
4. I can say and write the names of things in my classroom. ☐
5. I can say how many things I see. ☐
6. I can hear the number of syllables in words. ☐
7. I can greet people and say goodbye. ☐
8. I understand directions to the right and to the left. ☐

Unit 2 – Talking about People

 Listen. When we talk about <u>one person</u> we use these words:

| 1. man | 2. woman | 3. child | 4. boy | 5. girl |

✍ **Write**

1 _ _ _

2 _ _ _ _ _

3 _ _ _ _ _

 4. _ _ _

5. _ _ _ _

 Listen. When we talk about <u>two or more people</u> we use these words:

| 6. men | 7. women | 8. children |

✍ **Write**

6 _ _ _   7 _ _ _ _ _   8 _ _ _ _ _ _ _ _

How many men, women and children can you see in the picture?

There are two _____.   There are three _____.

There are five _____.

 Write answers to the questions.

How many men are in your class?   There are _____ in my class.

How many women are in your class?   There are _____ in my class.

How many people are in your class?   There are _____ in my class.

Family words

 Listen

| 1. wife | 2. mother | 3. husband | 4. father |
| 5. sister | 6. daughter | 7. brother | 8. son |

Write all the family words in the correct spaces.

 Listen

What are their <u>first names</u>?   What is their <u>surname</u> or <u>family name</u>?

____ ____ ____ ____   ____

 Highlight the family words.

m	o	t	h	e	r	h	f	q	y	w	i	f	e	l	e	b
b	u	c	r	o	l	l	a	s	c	a	a	t	c	h	m	o
s	i	s	t	e	r	a	t	h	e	o	r	s	t	p	w	r
t	i	u	n	g	k	u	h	r	e	b	r	o	t	h	e	r
o	c	o	u	s	i	n	e	o	w	t	t	n	i	c	x	t
d	a	u	g	h	t	e	r	x	q	h	u	s	b	a	n	d

The family words on this page are **nouns**.

English Language Skills - Level 1   19   www.boyereducation.com.au

More family words

Track 20 **Listen** and **read** the information about the Green family.

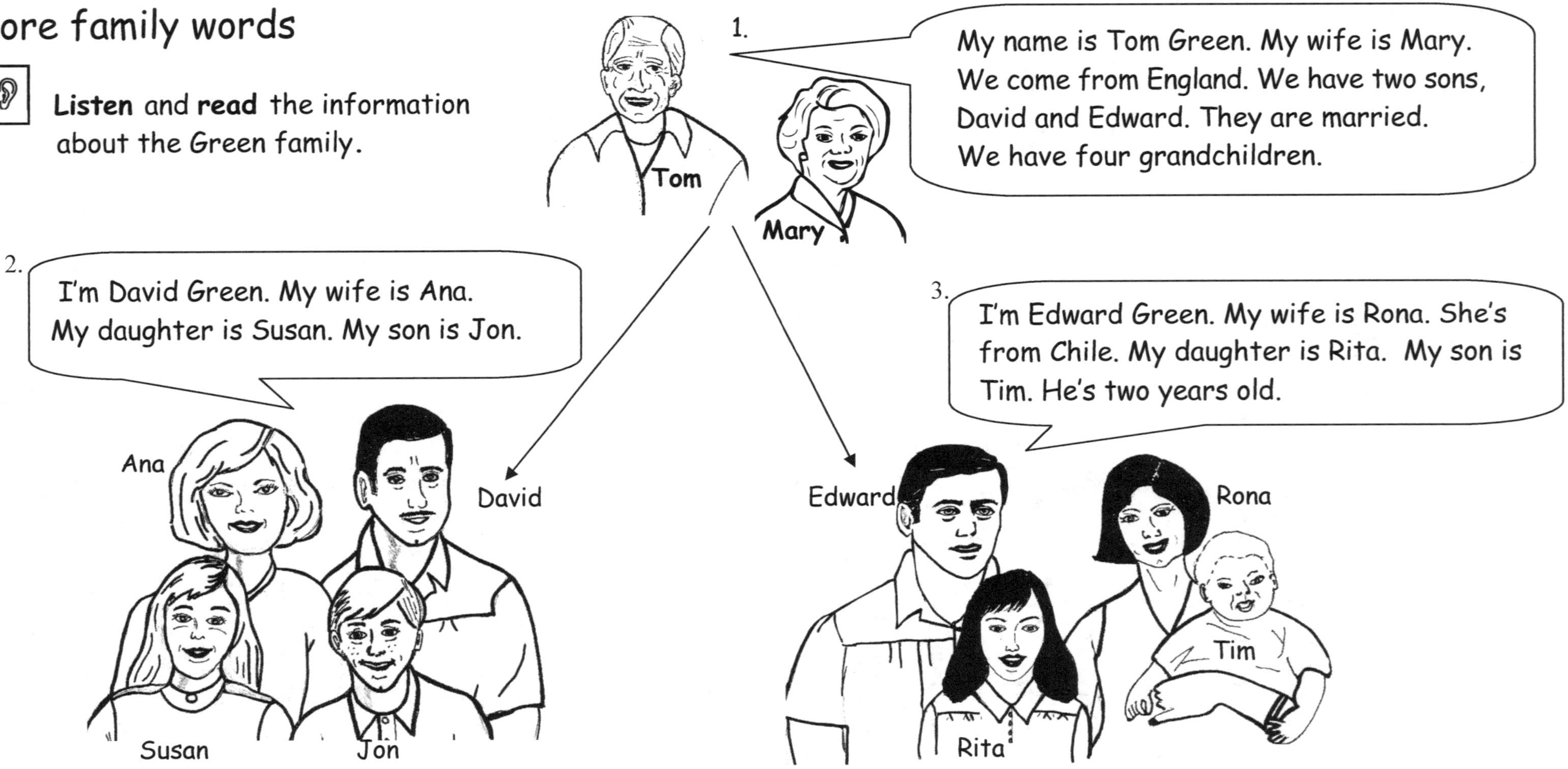

1. My name is Tom Green. My wife is Mary. We come from England. We have two sons, David and Edward. They are married. We have four grandchildren.

2. I'm David Green. My wife is Ana. My daughter is Susan. My son is Jon.

3. I'm Edward Green. My wife is Rona. She's from Chile. My daughter is Rita. My son is Tim. He's two years old.

When we speak, we use contractions for some words. This makes words shorter.

Track 21 **Listen**

I am	→	**I'm** David Green.
She is		**She's** from Chile.
He is		**He's** two years old.

I'm
She's
He's

 Highlight the contractions on this page.

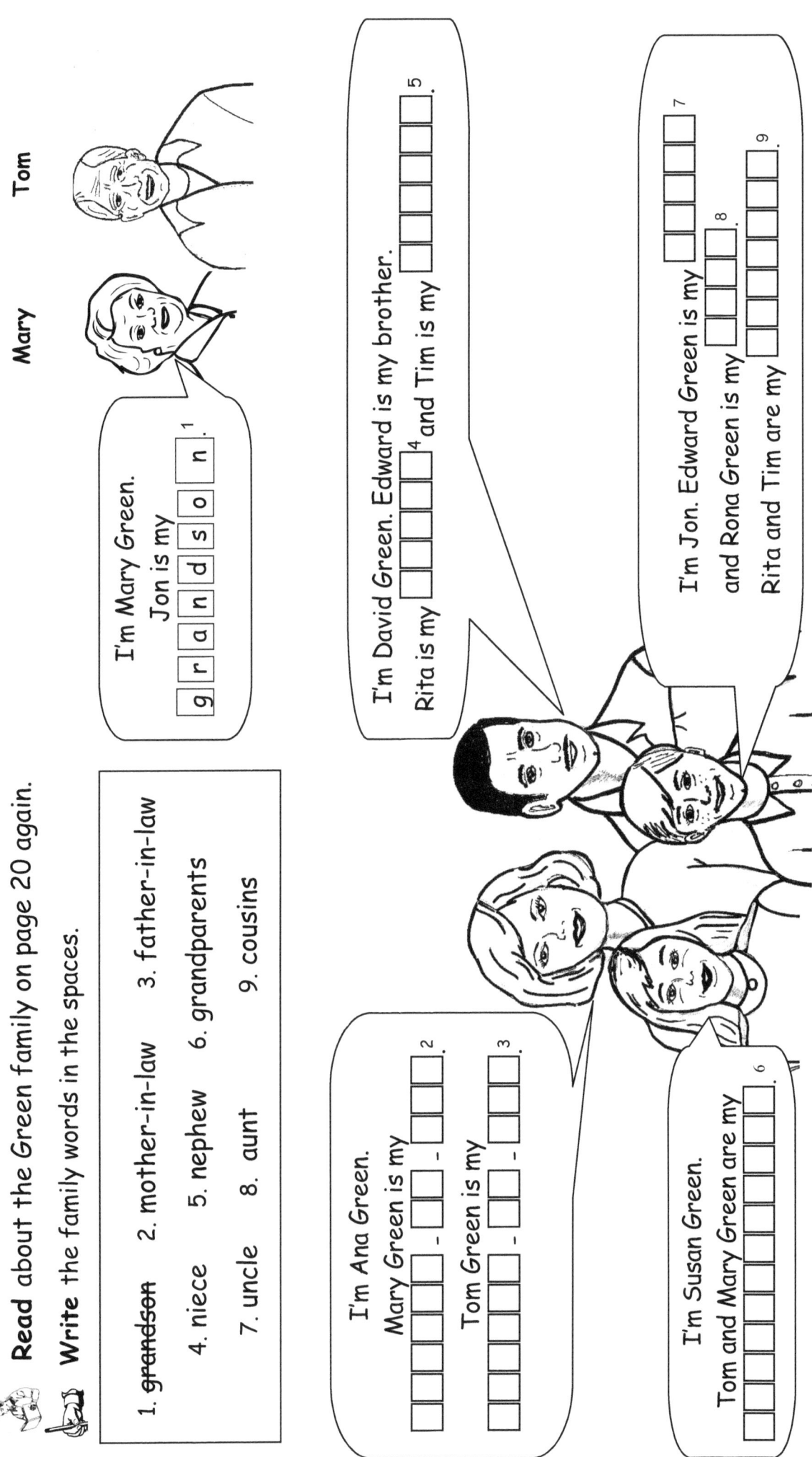

Read about the Green family on page 20 again.

Write the family words in the spaces.

1. ~~grandson~~ 2. mother-in-law 3. father-in-law
4. niece 5. nephew 6. grandparents
7. uncle 8. aunt 9. cousins

I'm Mary Green. Jon is my g r a n d s o n ¹.

I'm David Green. Edward is my brother. Rita is my ⁴ and Tim is my ⁵.

I'm Jon. Edward Green is my ⁷ and Rona Green is my ⁸. Rita and Tim are my ⁹.

I'm Ana Green. Mary Green is my ² . Tom Green is my ³ .

I'm Susan Green. Tom and Mary Green are my ⁶.

Track 22 **Listen** and check your answers. Learn the spelling of the family words. Your teacher will give you a **spelling test** on family words.

English Language Skills - Level 1

Giving information about me

We use names for people, places and things to give information.

 Write the words about Susan in the correct spaces.

| 1. Susan | 2. Australia | 3. dogs | 4. brother | 5. student |

1. My name is S u s a n .

2. I come from ☐☐☐☐☐☐☐☐☐ .

3. I like ☐☐☐☐ .

4. I have a ☐☐☐☐☐☐☐ .

5. I am a ☐☐☐☐☐☐☐ .

The words you have put in the boxes are all <u>nouns</u>.
Nouns are names of people, places and things.

 Write the sentences about Susan next to the pictures.

1. *My name is Susan.* _____

2. _____

3. _____

4. _____

5. _____

English Language Skills - Level 1

Write sentences about <u>you</u>.

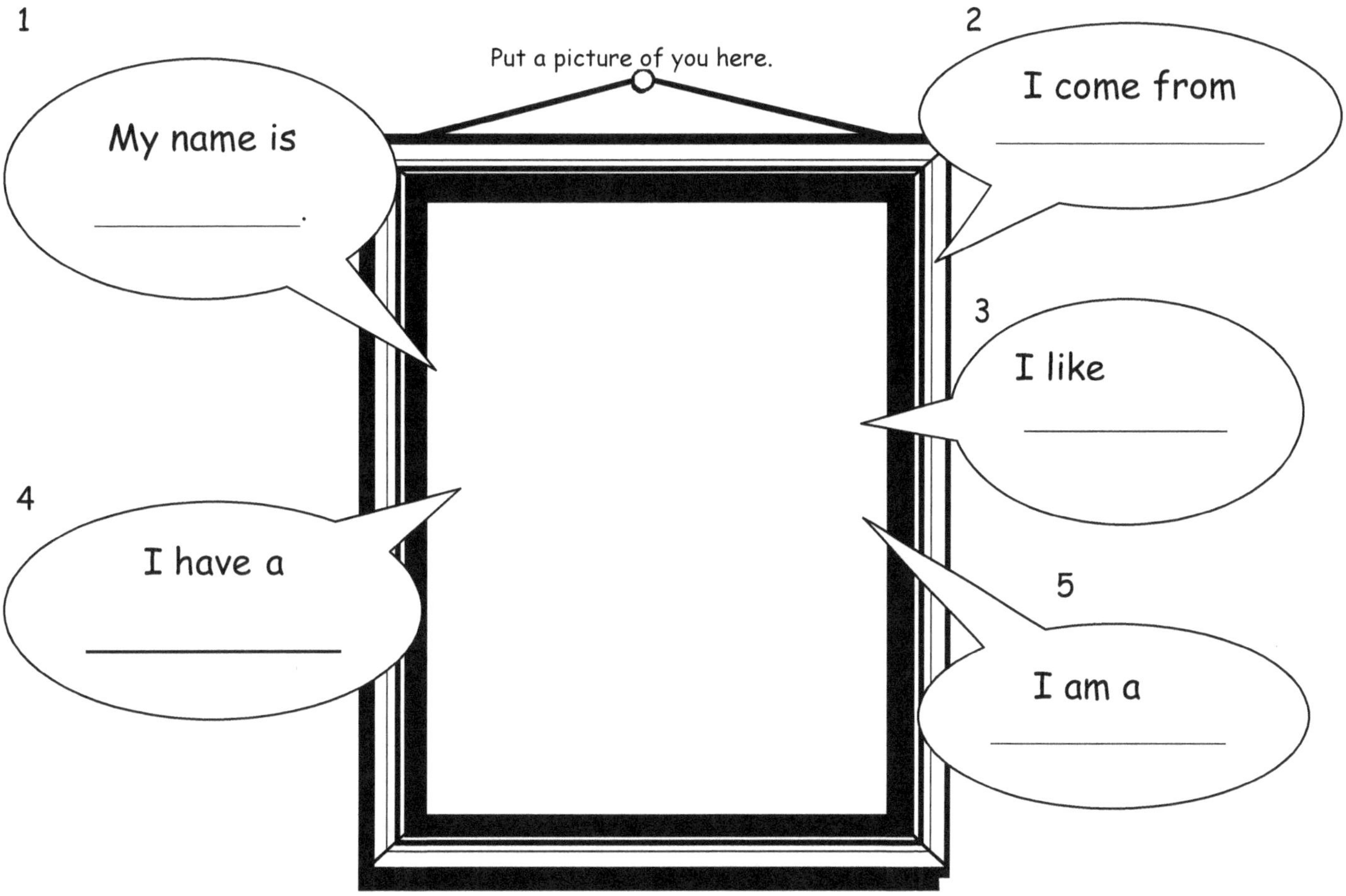

1 My name is _____.

Put a picture of you here.

2 I come from _____

3 I like _____

4 I have a _____

5 I am a _____

 Now write your sentences here.

Put a circle around the (nouns)

 **Listen** and **read** about Rona Green.

Rona Green

My name is Rona Green.
I have two children. My daughter, Rita, is ten years old.
My son, Tim, is two years old. I speak Spanish
because I come from Chile, in South America.

Chile →

I teach Spanish to other people every Monday morning.
On Monday I take my son, Tim, to Kindy Childcare Centre.
He is happy because he likes playing with other children.

Kindy Childcare Centre

 Highlight all the words in the story with capital letters.

A form

Rona must write information on
a form at the Childcare Centre.

Driver Licence
Rona Green
268 King Road
Hopetown 2999
Licence No
44332K1
Date of Birth
25 July 1980

Card No.
2010536895

Licence expires
22 Jun 2018

Rona Green

 Use the information from the story and Rona's driver licence
to write information on the form.

Childcare Centre Form	
Family name:	Name of mother: Name of child:
Address: Suburb:	Postcode:

Name and address

Rona wants to send a letter to Kindy Childcare Centre.

The address is: 386 Main Street
                  Hopetown 2999

front
back

✎ Write the address of the Childcare Centre on the front of this envelope.

Write the name here: *Kindy Childcare Centre*
Write the number and street here: _____
Write the suburb here: _____
Write the postcode here: ☐☐☐☐

✎ Write Rona's name and address on the back of the envelope.

Your teacher will give you more practice writing addresses.

Giving information about other people

Read the information with your teacher.   **Write:** He, She or It

1. When we introduce other people we say: *This is* ...

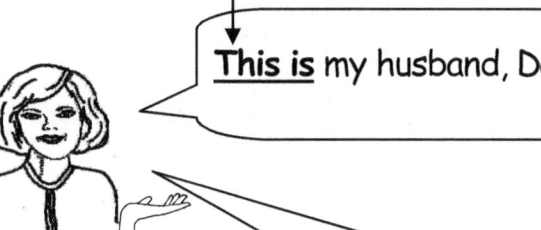

2. When we give information about a <u>boy</u> or a <u>man</u> we say: <u>*He*</u> *is*... ⟶

_____ is a teacher.

3. When we give information about a <u>girl</u> or <u>woman</u> we say: <u>*She*</u> *is*...

This is my friend, Rita.
_____ **is** from South America.

4. When we give information about a thing or place we say: <u>*It is*</u>...

This is my reading book.
_____ **is** interesting.

We use <u>he</u> and <u>she</u> to talk about **people**,
We use <u>it</u> to talk about **places** or **things**.

Talk about people in your class.

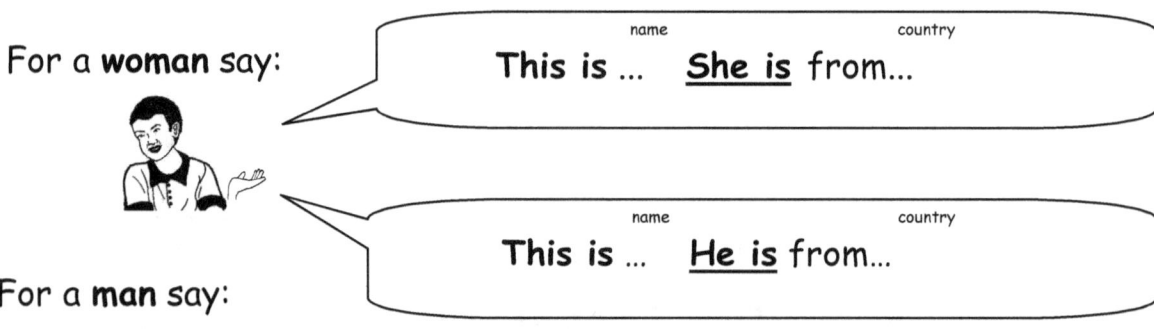

For a **woman** say: This is ...   <u>**She is**</u> from...

For a **man** say: This is ...   <u>**He is**</u> from...

Describing People

 Listen and read. Write: He or She

1. This is Rita. _She_ has short, straight, black hair.

2. This is Susan. _____ has long, straight, blonde hair.

3. This is Jo. _____ has short, curly black hair.

4. This is Omar. _____ has dark skin and a big smile. He is bald.

5. This is Bella. _____ has long, wavy blonde hair.

6. This is Boris. _____ has fair skin and short, blonde hair.

7. This is Ali. _____ has a moustache. _____ is wearing a cap.

8. This is Yasmin. _____ is wearing a scarf.

9. This is Tejinder. _____ has a moustache and a beard. _____ is wearing a turban.

 Write:

beard	moustache
curly	long	straight
blonde	short

10. This is Mohamed. He has a _____ and a _____

11. This is Rene. She has _____ black hair.

12. This is Michelle. She has _____, _____ black hair.

13. This is Karl. He has curly _____ hair.

14. This is David. He has _____ black hair.

 Write: I have _____

English Language Skills - Level 1

Describing people – clothes

 Listen.

| 1. tracksuits | 2. shoes | 3. cap | 4. T-shirt | 5. jeans | 6. skirt |
| 7. boots | 8. sunglasses | 9. hat | 10. shorts | 11. sandals |

Write

This is Ray and Pam. They are wearing _ _ _ _ _ _ _ _ _ _ ¹ and running _ _ _ _ _ _ ².

This is Rob. He is wearing a _ _ _ _ ³ and a _ _ - _ _ _ _ _ _ ⁴ and _ _ _ _ _ _ ⁵.

This is Sally. She is wearing a blouse and a _ _ _ _ _ _ ⁶ and _ _ _ _ _ _ ⁷.

This is Con. He is wearing _ _ _ _ _ _ _ _ _ _ _ ⁸.

This is Lily. She is wearing a _ _ _ _ ⁹ and a T-shirt and _ _ _ _ _ _ _ ¹⁰ and _ _ _ _ _ _ _ _ ¹¹.

Listen and read words for describing people.

| 1. tall | 2. thin | 3. young | 4. bald | 5. overweight | 6. short | 7. middle-aged |

Write

This is Jong. He is _ _ _ _ _ ¹, _ _ _ _ _ ² and _ _ _ _ _ _ ³.

This is Lee. He is _ _ _ _ _ ⁴. He is _ _ _ _ _ _ _ _ _ _ _ _ ⁵.

This is Wei. She is _ _ _ _ _ _ ⁶.

Lee and Wei are _ _ _ _ _ _ _ - _ _ _ _ ⁷.

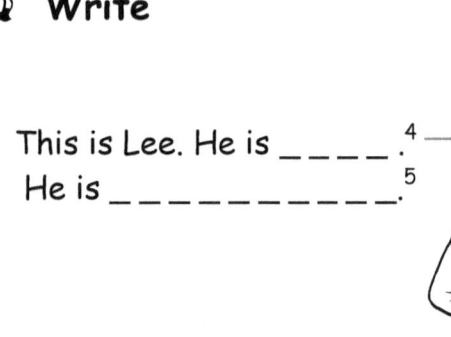

Talking about other people - photographs

We can say *This is...* to talk about one person, thing or place in a photograph.
We say *They are...* to talk about two or more people or things.

Listen to friends talking about photographs.

Write *is* or *are* in the conversation.

Ann: This is my sister's wedding.
      It is in my garden.

Tim: Really? It looks beautiful.

Ann: Thank you.
      And this is a photo of my friends, Ken and Lin.
      They _____ from China. They _____ students in my class.

Tim: They look friendly.

Ann: Yes, they _____. And this is a photo of my
      class party. This _____ my teacher here.

Tim: Yes, I see. And where is this?

Ann: This _____ my house here.
      And this _____ my dog.

Practise the conversation with another person.

Words and sounds

Listen.

One word has a different vowel sound. Circle the different word.

b<u>oo</u>t   sh<u>oe</u>s   d<u>o</u>g   tw<u>o</u>   y<u>ou</u>

English Language Skills - Level 1   29   © Boyer Educational Resources

Asking questions

We use special words to ask questions when we want information.

We use **Who**  to ask about **people**.   We use **What**  to ask about **things**.   We use **Where**  to ask about **places**.

✏️ Write: **Who**, **What** or **Where**

1. _____ is this?   2. _____ is this?   3. _____ is this?

4. _____ is this?   5. _____ is this?   6. _____ is this?

Look at some photographs.
Ask questions about the photographs.

Who is this?   **Where is this?**   **What is this?**

Talking about other people

When we talk about people we use their <u>name</u> in the first sentence.
After that we can use the words: **he, she, they, it** (pronouns).

Names:  Tom   Mary   Mary and Tom   Glenbrook

Pronouns: ➝ he   she   they   it

✏️ Write **he, she, they,** or **it** in the sentences.

The pronoun for a man is _ _
The pronoun for a woman is _ _ _
The pronoun for <u>more than one</u> person is _ _ _ _
The pronoun for a place is _ _

English Language Skills - Level 1

Using Pronouns: He, she, they, it

 **Listen** and read the story about Mary and Tom.

 Highlight the pronouns *She, He, They* and *It*.

Mary and Tom Green

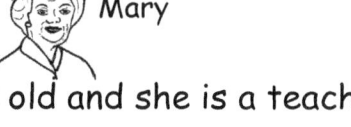

This is Mary Green. She is 59 years old and she is a teacher. She is married to Tom. He is a gardener. He likes his job because he likes working outside.

Mary Green and Tom Green have been married for forty years. They have four grandchildren. They live in a place called Glenbrook. It is a small town in the mountains.

 Write the story about Jane and Mike with the pronouns:
he, she, they or *it* where you see lines.

Jane and Mike

This is Jane. _____ (Jane) is 34 years old and _____ (Jane) is a teacher.

_____ (Jane) is married to Mike. _____ (Mike) is a mechanic. _____ (Mike) likes his job because _____ (Mike) likes cars.

Jane and Mike have been married for ten years. _____ (Jane and Mike) have two children. _____ (Jane and Mike) live in a place called Newtown. _____ (Newtown) is a busy place near the city.

 **Listen** to the story about Jane and Mike. Check the pronouns.

Saying English words - syllables

Track 31 Listen to syllables in the words.

One-syllable words	Two-syllable words	Three-syllable words
son wife child	children husband cousin	grand pa rents grand mo ther

Listen. How many syllables are in each word?

Write 1, 2 or 3.

niece	1	→	mother	☐	→	women	☐
father	☐		nephew	☐		grandson	☐
daughter	☐		brother	☐		grandfather	☐

Syllables and Word Stress

Track 32 Listen to these words with two syllables.

Can you hear that the <u>first syllable</u> is <u>louder and longer</u>?

• ·   • ·   • ·
<u>tea</u>cher   <u>daugh</u>ter   <u>peo</u>ple

Listen to these words with two syllables.

Which syllable is louder and longer?

student   garden   father   question

In words with two or more syllables, we say one syllable **louder** and **longer**. This is called **word stress**.

Mark the stress on the <u>first</u> syllable of these words:

children   husband   cousin   grandmother

Listen to **Track 31** again. Say the words.

Giving information - Using verbs

When we give information, every sentence has a <u>verb</u>.

Track 33 **Listen** and **read** the sentences about Ana. The verbs are <u>underlined</u>.

Write a <u>verb</u> in each sentence about David.

| is | come | like | have | am |

Look at your sentences on page 23. <u>Underline</u> a verb in each sentence.

English Language Skills - Level 1

Unit 3 - Everyday activities

On page 33 you learnt about verbs. When we give information every sentence has a verb. Underline the verbs in the sentences about Kara.

Kara   My name is Kara. I come from Spain. I have two sons. I am a nurse in a big hospital. I like computer games.

We use verbs to tell about the things we do.

 Listen and write a verb under each picture.

walk	cook	watch	write	drive
sing	listen	drink	read	shop

a. _____   b. _walk_   c. _____   d. _____   e. _____

f. _____   g. _____   h. _____   i. _____   j. _____

In each sentence, draw a line under the verb.

1. I walk in the park.
2. I cook my food.
3. I watch TV with my family.
4. I write a letter.
5. I drive to the city.
6. I sing a song.
7. I listen on the telephone.
8. I drink tea in a mug.
9. I read my book.
10. I shop for food and other things.

Write the underlined verbs next to the numbers.

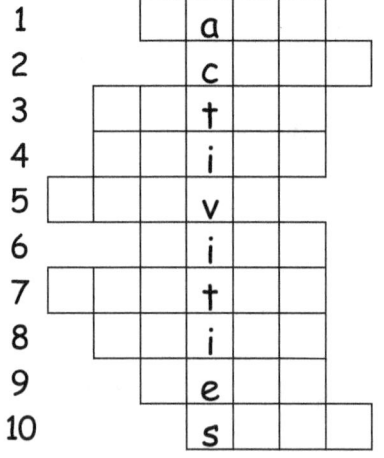

Write a verb in each sentence.

| walk | cook | watch | write | drive |
| sing | listen | drink | read | shop |

1. I _____ in the park with my friend.
2. I _____ food for my friends.
3. I _____ a movie on TV with my family.
4. I _____ emails to my friends.
5. I _____ to the city every day.
6. I _____ a song when I am happy.
7. I _____ to my friend on the phone.
8. I _____ water every day.
9. I _____ my book in bed.
10. I _____ for food and other things on Friday.

Can you swim?

We put 'can' or 'can't' before a verb to say things we can do and can't do.

I **can** drive  but I **can't** cook.

I **can** dance  but I **can't** swim.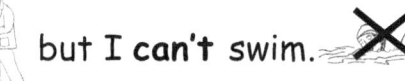

can't means
can not

We ask questions and give short answers with <u>can</u> or <u>can't</u>.

Track 35

Listen to Kate and John talking about things they <u>can</u> do and <u>can't</u> do.

Kate:	Hey John. Can you drive?
John:	Yes, I can.
Kate:	Can you cook?
John:	No, I can't.
	OK. Now I'll ask you questions. Can you cook?
Kate:	Yes, I can.
John:	Can you swim?
Kate:	Yes, I can.
John:	Can you speak Chinese?
Kate:	No, I can't.

  Practise the conversation.

What can John and Kate do?

Write

John can_____ but he can't _____.

Kate can _____ and _____ but she can't _____.

What can <u>you</u> do?

Listen

| 1. draw | 2. ride a bicycle | 3. play the guitar |
| 4. sew | 5. use a computer | 6. play cards |

Write the words below the pictures.

a. _____   b. <u>use a computer</u>   c. _____

d. _____   e. _____   f. _____

Write four sentences about what <u>you can do</u>.

<u>I can speak</u> _____

_____

_____

_____

Ask other students questions beginning with: **Can you** ....

Talking about activities we like doing

We put '**ing**' at the end of some verbs to talk about activities.

 Listen to these activities:

| shopping | walking | reading | cooking | singing |
| watching | visiting | talking | cleaning |

We can talk about things we **like doing** and things we **don't like doing**.

 Listen and read the story about Rita.

Highlight all the activities that end in '**ing**'.

My name is Rita. I like shopping with my husband, Jack.
I like visiting my friends and talking about our children.
I like driving near my home but I don't like driving in busy places.
I like watching funny movies on TV but I don't like watching sad movies.
I like reading emails from my friends but I don't like writing emails.
I like cooking but I don't like cleaning the kitchen.

Read the story about Rita again.

 Write what Rita says.

I like…   I **don't** like…

_____   _____

_____   _____

_____   _____

Ask your teacher about a word you don't understand.

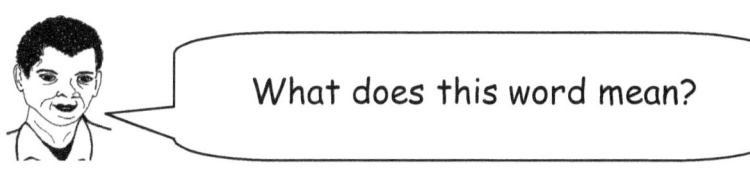

What does this word mean?

What do you like doing?

Track 39 **Listen** to the names of the activities.

fishing	cycling	running	sewing
swimming	playing games	flying	
dancing	watching sport	drawing	

Write the activities below the pictures.

a. _____ b. _____ c. _____ d. _____

e. _____ f. _____ g. _____ h. _____

i. _____ j. _____

What do you like doing?

Write sentences about activities you like doing.

I like _____

_____

_____

Write sentences about activities you **don't** like doing.

I don't like _____

_____

_____

English Language Skills - Level 1

Jobs

Listen to the jobs.

| builder | mechanic | chef | plumber | teacher |
| cleaner | electrician | hairdresser | shop assistant |

Write the jobs below the pictures.

a. _____ b. _____ c. _____

d. _____ e. _____ f. _____

g. _____ h. _____ i. _____

Write a job in each sentence.

1. A _____ builds houses.
2. A _____ repairs cars.
3. A _____ cooks food.
4. A _____ repairs toilets.
5. A _____ teaches people.
6. A _____ cleans places.
7. An _____ repairs electrical things.
8. A _____ cuts hair.
9. A _____ _____ sells things.

Write

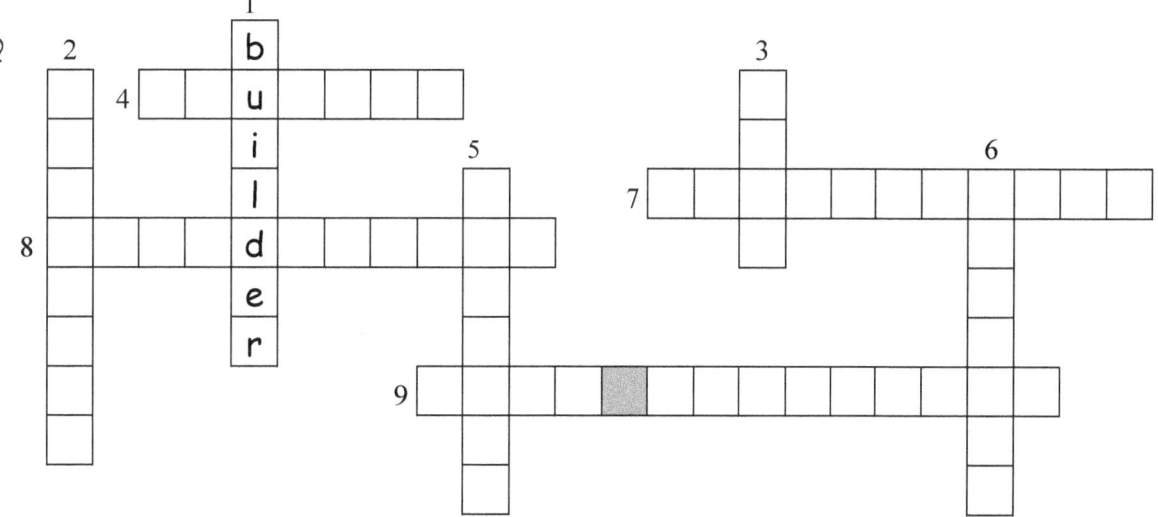

What do people do in their jobs?

Verbs tell us what people <u>do</u> in their jobs.
Underline the verbs in the sentences on page 39.

When we say what <u>other people</u> do we put **s** or **es** at the end of the verb.

Write a verb with 's' or 'es' in each sentence to tell what the people do.

1. A builder _____ houses.

2. A mechanic _____ cars.

3. A chef _____ food.

4. A plumber _____ toilets and water pipes.

5. A teacher _____ people.

6. A cleaner _____ places.

7. An electrician _____ electrical things.

8. A hairdresser _____ hair.

9. A shop assistant _____ things.

When we write about **he**, **she** or **it**, we write **s** or **es** at the end of the verb.

 Listen and read this story about Tim. Find and highlight 15 verbs.

Tim is a cleaner. He cleans buildings and windows six days each week. He gets up early and has a quick breakfast. Then he drives to the city.

When he is very busy, his sister Jill helps him. Jill washes the windows and Tim sweeps the floors. At the end of a busy day he thanks her very much. He tells her she is a very good sister. She smiles and says he is a good brother too.

What does Tim do?   What does Jill do?

Listen to the verbs. Which word has two syllables?

| cleans | drives | helps | washes | has |
| thanks | | smiles | | tells |

Find and highlight the verbs.

v	s	m	i	l	e	s	h	t	w	x	c	l	e	a	n	s
n	w	u	c	r	o	l	k	y	s	c	l	a	e	c	h	e
s	m	n	g	x	l	h	e	l	p	s	o	d	a	h	a	q
h	a	s	m	n	g	k	a	x	r	d	r	i	v	e	s	t
d	o	e	s	t	h	a	n	k	s	w	g	t	e	l	l	s
w	a	s	h	e	s	g	w	l	e	q	r	l	l	x	m	y

Read the story about Tim again and highlight **ten** mistakes with verbs.

Tim is a cleaner. He clean buildings and windows six days each week. He get up early and has a quick breakfast. Then he drive to the city.

When he is very busy, his sister Jill help him. Jill wash the windows and Tim sweep the floors. At the end of a busy day he thank her very much. He tell her she is a very good sister. She smile and say he is a good brother too.

Write the story with the correct verbs.

Read the story aloud, saying the verbs correctly with 's' or 'es' at the end.

Stories about other people

Track 43 **Listen** and read the story about Mai. Highlight the verbs.

This **is** Mai. She comes from Vietnam. Now she lives in New Zealand. She is twenty-two years old.
She is a shop assistant. She works on Friday and Saturday.

Mai goes to English classes on Monday, Wednesday and Thursday. She likes singing and dancing.

Read the questions about Mai. **Write** the answers.

1. Where does Mai come from?

1. _____ comes from _____

2. How old is Mai?

2. _____ is _____ years old.

3. Where does Mai live now?

3. Now _____ lives in _____

4. What does Mai do?

4. She is a _____ _____.

5. When does Mai work?

5. She works on _____

6. What does Mai like doing?

6. _____ likes _____ and _____.

7. When does Mai go to English classes?

7. She _____

What does Mai look like? Write the correct words in the sentences.

| curly, blonde | straight, black | young | middle-aged |

Mai has_____hair. She is _____.

Writing about other people

Write a story about the person in the picture.

- What is the name of the person?
- Where does the person come from?
- Where does the person live now?
- How old is the person?
- What does the person do?
- What days does the person work or study?
- What does the person like doing?

This is _____

_____

_____

_____

_____

_____

_____

_____

_____

Words and sounds

Track 44 Listen.

One word has a different vowel sound. Circle the different word.

w<u>a</u>tch   wh<u>a</u>t   w<u>a</u>sh   d<u>o</u>   sh<u>o</u>p

Unit 4 - Talking about time and events

Track 45 **Listen** to these words. We use them to talk about time.

| hours | day | week | month | year | o'clock |
| noon | | morning | | afternoon | weekend |

✎ Write the words in the correct place to show the meaning

1. There are 24 _____ in a _____.

2. There are 7 days in a _____.

3. There are 4 weeks in a _____.

4. There are 52 weeks in each _____.

5. _____ is used to show the hour in time.

6. _____ means 12 o'clock in the middle of the day.

7. _____ means before noon.

8. _____ means after noon.

9. _____ means Saturday and Sunday.

Track 46 **Listen** to the names of the days of the week. How many syllables in each word?

Monday 2 Tuesday___ Wednesday___ Thursday___ Friday___ Saturday___ Sunday___

✎ Write the name of the day to make true sentences.

Today is _____

Tomorrow is _____

The day after tomorrow is_____

Yesterday was _____

Months of the Year

Track 47 Listen to the names of the 12 months of the year.

1. January	2. February	3. March	4. April	5. May
6. June	7. July	8. August	9. September	
10. October	11. November	12. December		

English Language Skills - Level 1

Write the twelve months of the year

1. J__ __ __ __ __ y
2. F__ __ __ __ __ __ y
3. M__ __ ch
4. A__ __ __ __
5. M__ __
6. J__ __ e
7. J __ __ y

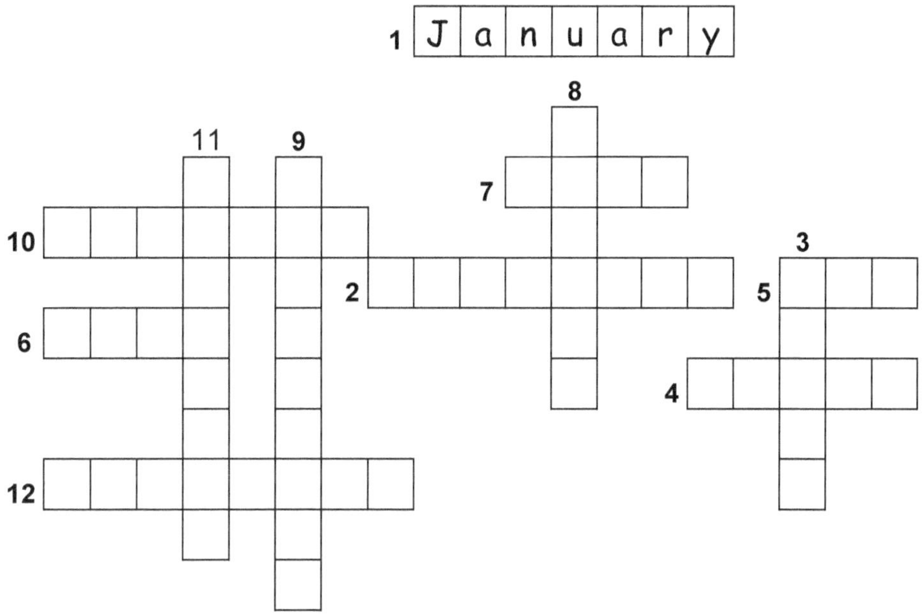

1 | J | a | n | u | a | r | y |

8. A __ __ __ __ __ __
9. S__ __ __ __ __ __ er
10. O __ __ __ __ __ er
11. N __ __ __ __ __ er
12. D__ __ __ __ __ er

Write the names of the months in each season where you live.

Summer 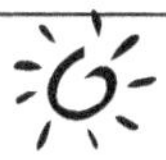	Autumn 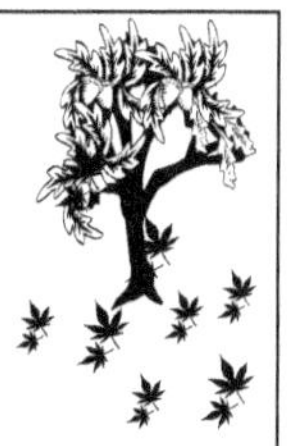
Winter 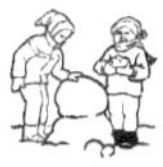	Spring 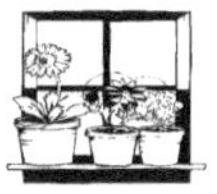

How many **syllables** are in the name of each month?

Write 1, 2, 3 or 4

January	4 →	February → ☐	March ☐	April ☐
May ☐	June ☐	July ☐	August ☐
September ☐	October ☐	November ☐	December ☐

What is the date?

We can write dates with <u>numbers only</u> or with <u>numbers and words</u>

Date with numbers	Date with numbers and words
date month year	date month year
25 / 07 / 2009	25th July 2009

✏️ Write the dates with numbers and with numbers and words.

Today _____   _____

Your birthday _____   _____

When is your birthday?

Ask: When is your birthday?

Put a tick ✓ next to the month each person says.

Month	✓	How many?	Month	✓	How many?
January			July		
February			August		
March			September		
April			October		
May			November		
June			December		

Write a number for how many ticks you have put next to each month.

Show the information on a graph

- Fill squares with colour to the number of ticks for each month.
- Use a different colour for each month.

10												
9												
8												
7												
6												
5												
4												
3												
2												
1												
	Jan	Feb	March	April	May	June	July	Aug	Sept	Oct	Nov	Dec

Which month has the most birthdays? _____

English Language Skills - Level 1   © Boyer Educational Resources

What is the time?

| What is the time now? Put the time on the clock. | Write the time with numbers. | Write the time with words. |

   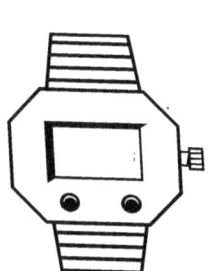   It is _____

Talking about routine

Routine means the things we do and <u>when</u> we do them.

 Listen and read the story about Jack's routine.

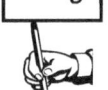 Write numbers to show the time.

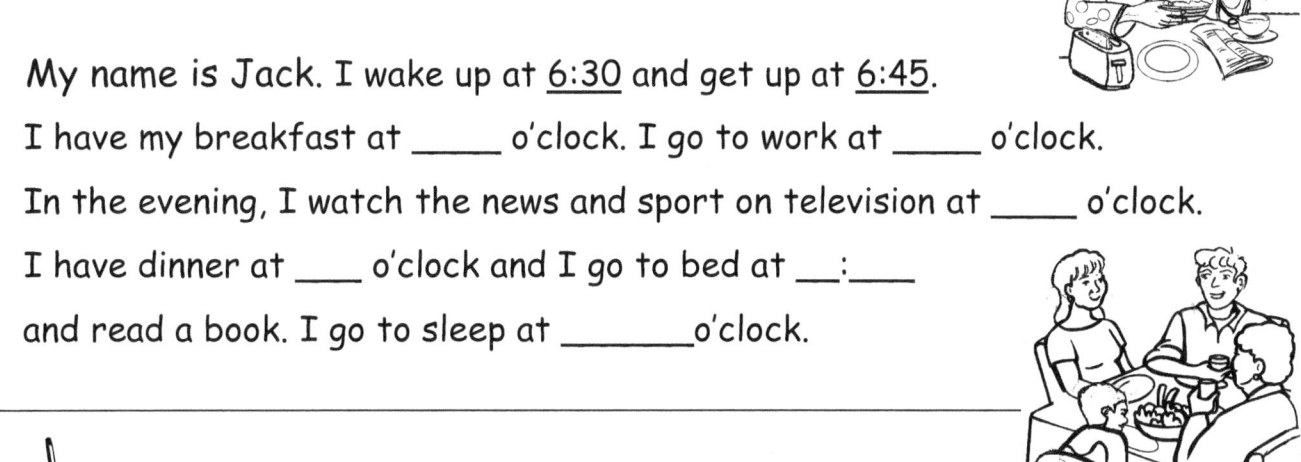

My name is Jack. I wake up at <u>6:30</u> and get up at <u>6:45</u>.

I have my breakfast at _____ o'clock. I go to work at _____ o'clock.

In the evening, I watch the news and sport on television at _____ o'clock.

I have dinner at ____ o'clock and I go to bed at __:___

and read a book. I go to sleep at _____ o'clock.

 Write **your** routine.

<u>I wake up at</u> _____

_____

_____

_____

_____

English Language Skills - Level 1

Boris and Natasha's routine

 **Listen** and read the story about Boris and Natasha.

Underline the verbs in the story. Remember *is* and *am* are verbs.

(I'm = I am)

Boris and Natasha

My name <u>is</u> Boris and my wife's name <u>is</u> Natasha. My wife <u>works</u> in a shop and I'<u>m</u> a mechanic. Every afternoon we walk in the park with our dog. We always go to English class on Monday night.

We often meet with friends on Friday night. Usually we eat dinner together and sometimes we watch a movie. On Saturday we clean the house and the garden. On Sunday we usually go out somewhere. Sometimes we go for a picnic by the river. Sometimes we go to the beach. We never work on Sunday because it is our day off.

Write answers to the questions about Boris' and Natasha's routine.

1. When do Boris and Natasha go to the park?_____
2. When do they go to English classes? _____
3. When do they meet with friends? _____
4. What do they do on Saturday? _____
5. What do they do on Sunday?_____

Saying when we do things

When we say <u>how often</u> we do things, we use these words:

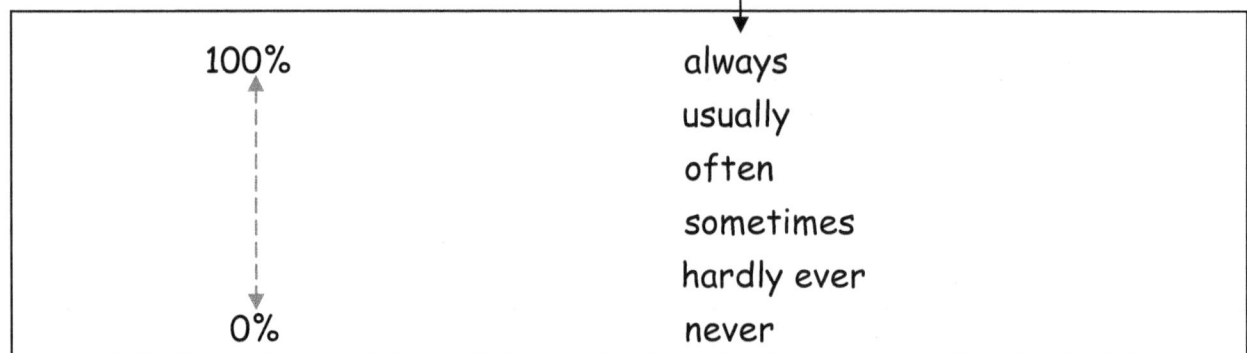

Highlight words that show <u>when</u> Boris and Natasha do things.

Words and sounds

Listen. One word has a different vowel sound. Circle the different word.

w<u>i</u>fe   l<u>i</u>ke   d<u>i</u>d   n<u>i</u>ght   t<u>i</u>me   dr<u>i</u>ve

How often?

When someone asks **how often** we do an activity, we can say **how many times**.

How often do you walk in the park?

I walk in the park <u>once a week</u> (one time in a week)
I walk in the park <u>twice a week</u> (two times in a week)
I walk in the park <u>three times a week</u>.
I walk in the park <u>every day</u>.

Saying <u>when</u> we do things

 Put a line under the <u>verbs</u> and words that explain <u>how often</u>.

1. I <u>always drink</u> tea in the morning.
2. I often cook Chinese food.
3. I never write emails to my friends.
4. I often drive to the city.
5. I usually listen to music in the car.
6. Sometimes I watch the news on TV.
7. I shop for food and other things once a week.
8. I walk to my English class every day.

 Write how often <u>you</u> do these things.

How often do you drink coffee? _____

How often do you walk to the shops? _____

How often do you go to the beach? _____

How often do you **cook dinner**? _____

How often do you **shop for food**? _____

 Ask the questions with other people in your class.

Past, present and future time

We use different words to talk about **past** time, **present** time and **future** time.

Write the words under **past**, **present** or **future**

past time	present time	future time
now yesterday did tomorrow last month next month at present last year next year will		

Asking questions about the past

We <u>ask questions</u> about the past with '**did**'

    did + verb
    ↓   ↓

Did you **have** fish for breakfast?

We make short answers with **Yes, I did.**

    or

No, I didn't.

 Listen to the questions about the past.

Highlight **did** and the **verb**.   Tick ✓ the answer you hear.

1. Did you have fish for breakfast?   Yes, I did. ☐   No, I didn't. ☐
2. Did you watch TV last night?   Yes, I did. ☐   No, I didn't. ☐
3. Did you walk in the park yesterday?   Yes, I did. ☐   No, I didn't. ☐
4. Did you have a busy weekend?   Yes, I did. ☐   No, I didn't. ☐

 Ask and answer the questions with other people in your class.

Questions beginning with where, when, what, who

We can make questions about the past with **where, when, what, who**

           did   verb
           ↓   ↓

 Listen to the questions.   <u>Where</u> **did** you **live** last year?

 Highlight **did** and the **verb**.   <u>When</u> **did** you **start** your English class?

    <u>Who</u> **did** you **talk** to yesterday?

    <u>What</u> **did** you **play** as a child?

Giving information about the past

We write 'ed' on the end of some verbs to talk about the past.

Listen.
    present   past   present   past
    want → want**ed**   look → look**ed**

Write: Change the verbs to past tense by adding *ed*.

    cook _ _   listen_ _   walk _ _

We add 'd' to make past tense when a word ends with **e**:

    save → save**d**   smile → smile**d**

Write: Change the verbs to past tense by adding **d**.

    live_   like_   dance_

Syllables

Sometimes 'ed' makes another syllable. Usually it does **not**.

Listen and write <u>how many syllables</u> in each verb.

Write 1 or 2	walked	1	looked	☐	talked	☐
	missed	☐	liked	☐	worked	☐
	started	☐	needed	☐	wanted	☐

Listen to the questions and answers about the past.

Write the past tense verbs in the answers.

Questions	Answers
1. Where did you <u>live</u> last year?	I _____ in Italy.
2. When did you <u>start</u> your English class?	I _____ my English class in May.
3. Who did you <u>talk</u> to yesterday?	I _____ to my neighbour.
4. What did you <u>play</u> as a child?	I _____ ball games.

Ask and answer the questions with other people in your class.

Write a past tense verb in each sentence.

| walked | listened | cooked | shopped |
| watched | | played | |

a. Yesterday I _____ in the park with my friend.

b. Yesterday I _____ food for my friends.

c. Last night I _____ a movie on TV with my family.

d. Last night I _____ to music.

e. Yesterday I _____ for food and other things.

f. Last week I _____ cards with my friends.

Write the past tense verbs in the story about Mai's weekend.

| visited | walked | talked | cooked |
| listened | shopped | watched | played |

Listen to the story about Mai's weekend. (Track 55)

Mai's weekend

My name is Mai. Last weekend I _____ ¹ friends.

On Saturday morning we _____ ² to the park and _____ ³ for an hour. At lunchtime we _____ ⁴ a big plate of pancakes and _____ ⁵ to music. In the afternoon we _____ ⁶ for new clothes at the shopping centre. After dinner we _____ ⁷ a movie and then we _____ ⁸ games on the computer.

English Language Skills - Level 1

Write answers to the questions.

1. What did Mai and her friends do on Saturday morning?

1. They _____

2. What did they do at lunchtime?

2. _____

3. What did they do in the afternoon?

3. _____

4. What did they do after dinner?

4. _____

More past tense verbs

We change the spelling of <u>some</u> verbs when we talk about the past.

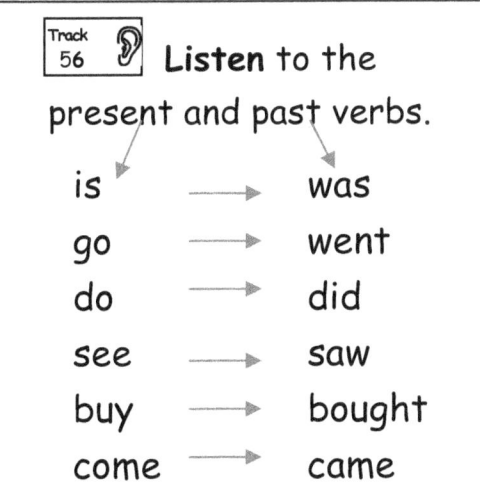

Highlight the past verbs.

1. Yesterday was hot.
2. I went to the supermarket yesterday.
3. I did my homework last night.
4. I saw a kangaroo last week.
5. Yesterday I bought new shoes.
6. We came to this country last year.

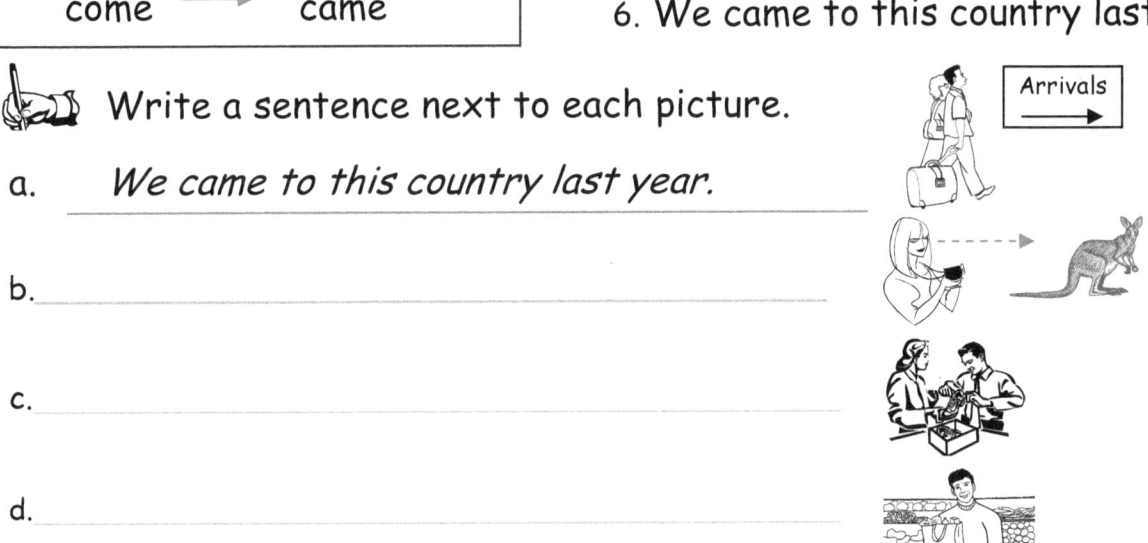

Write a sentence next to each picture.

a. *We came to this country last year.*

b. _____

c. _____

d. _____

e. _____

f. _____

57 Listen and read Jo's story.

Jo's Story

My name is Jo. When I was a child I lived in Africa on a farm. When I was sixteen I went to school in the city. I lived with my aunt and uncle for two years. I went to school with my cousins and saw many new things. After school I worked in my uncle's shop for two years.

When I was nineteen I bought a motorbike. On weekends I went to different places on my motorbike. Sometimes I went to the mountains. Sometimes I went to the beach.

Now I live in the city and I am a mechanic.

Highlight **all** the verbs. (Circle) the verbs about present time.

 Write sentences about Jo.

1. Where did Jo live when he was a child?

1. He _____

2. Where did he live for two years?

2. He lived with his _____

3. Where did he work for two years?

3. He worked in his _____

4. What did he buy when he was nineteen?

4. _____

5. Where did he go on weekends?

5. _____

Words and sounds

58 Listen.
One word has a different vowel sound. (Circle) the different word.

b<u>ou</u>ght   h<u>o</u>t   w<u>a</u>lk   t<u>a</u>lk   s<u>aw</u>

Past tense verbs

 Write the past tense of these verbs.

Present	Past	Present	Past	Present	Past
1. shop	shopped	5. play	_____	9. talk	_____
2. is	_____	6. see	_____	10. go	_____
3. buy	_____	7. come	_____	11. walk	_____
4. cook	_____	8. do	_____	12. live	_____

 Now write the **past tense verbs** next to the numbers.

 Write about you.

1. Where did you live last year?

   Last year I _____

2. Where did you go yesterday?

   Yesterday I _____

3. What did you see yesterday?

   Yesterday I _____

4. What did you buy yesterday?

   Yesterday I _____

 Ask other students.

Special days

Listen and read the story about Chinese New Year.

My name is Kim. Yesterday I went shopping. Today I am busy cooking and cleaning my house because tomorrow will be Chinese New Year. Tonight I will watch fireworks with my family. We will have a big dinner together. We will eat fish and vegetables. When the moon is full I will watch a lion dance, with my family. I like Chinese New year!

Write short answers.

1. What did Kim do yesterday? _____
2. What is Kim doing today? _____
3. In Kim's story, tomorrow will be what special day? _____
4. What will Kim do with her family? _____

More special days

| Christmas | New Year | birthday | Easter |
| engagement | wedding | funeral | |

Write names of the special days below the pictures.

1 _____ 2 _____ 3 _____ 4 _____

5 _____ 6 _____ 7 _____

✏️ Write the names of special days next to the numbers.

What about you?

1. What is the **name** of a special day in your culture?
2. In which **month** is the special day?
3. What do people **do** on the special days?

✏️ Write about your culture.

1. The name of the special time is _____

2. The special day is in the month of _____

3. On the special day, people _____

_____

Words and sounds

🎧 Listen.

One word has a different vowel sound. (Circle) the different word.

noon   June   month   do   moon

English Language Skills - Level 1   57   © Boyer Educational Resources

Bob's story

 Listen and read Bob's story.

Write the verbs in the story.

| ~~is~~ | had | came |
| cooked | was | cooked |

My name is Bob. On Saturday we _____ a barbecue in our garden. I _____ the meat and my wife _____ the vegetables. Many friends _____ to our house. It _____ a very good day.

Bella's story

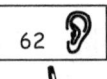 Listen and read Bella's story.

 Write all the verbs in the story.

| was | bought | went |
| went | was | watched |

My name is Bella. Yesterday _____ my birthday. I _____ to the city with my friends. They _____ my lunch at a café and then we _____ to the cinema and _____ a movie. It _____ a very good day.

Our holiday

 Listen. Highlight all the past tense verbs in the story. There are 10.

Last week we went to our friend's house for a holiday. On Monday we played cards in the afternoon. On Tuesday we walked in the park and saw some ducks. On Wednesday we stayed home and worked in the garden. On Thursday we went for a ride on our bicycles. On Friday we watched a funny movie on TV. On Saturday we had a barbecue in the garden. On Sunday we went home.

Write the <u>day</u> under each picture.

a._____ b._____ c._____

d _____ e _____

f _____ g _____

Words and sounds

 Listen.

One word has a different vowel sound. Circle the different word.

c<u>a</u>rds   g<u>a</u>rden   b<u>a</u>rbecue   f<u>a</u>rm   p<u>a</u>rk   h<u>a</u>d

Unit 5 - Health and safety

🔊 **65** Listen and read the names for parts of the body.

1. head →	2. hair	3. neck	4. shoulders
5. chest	6. back	7. stomach	8. arms
9. hands	10. fingers	11. legs	12. feet

✏️ **Write**

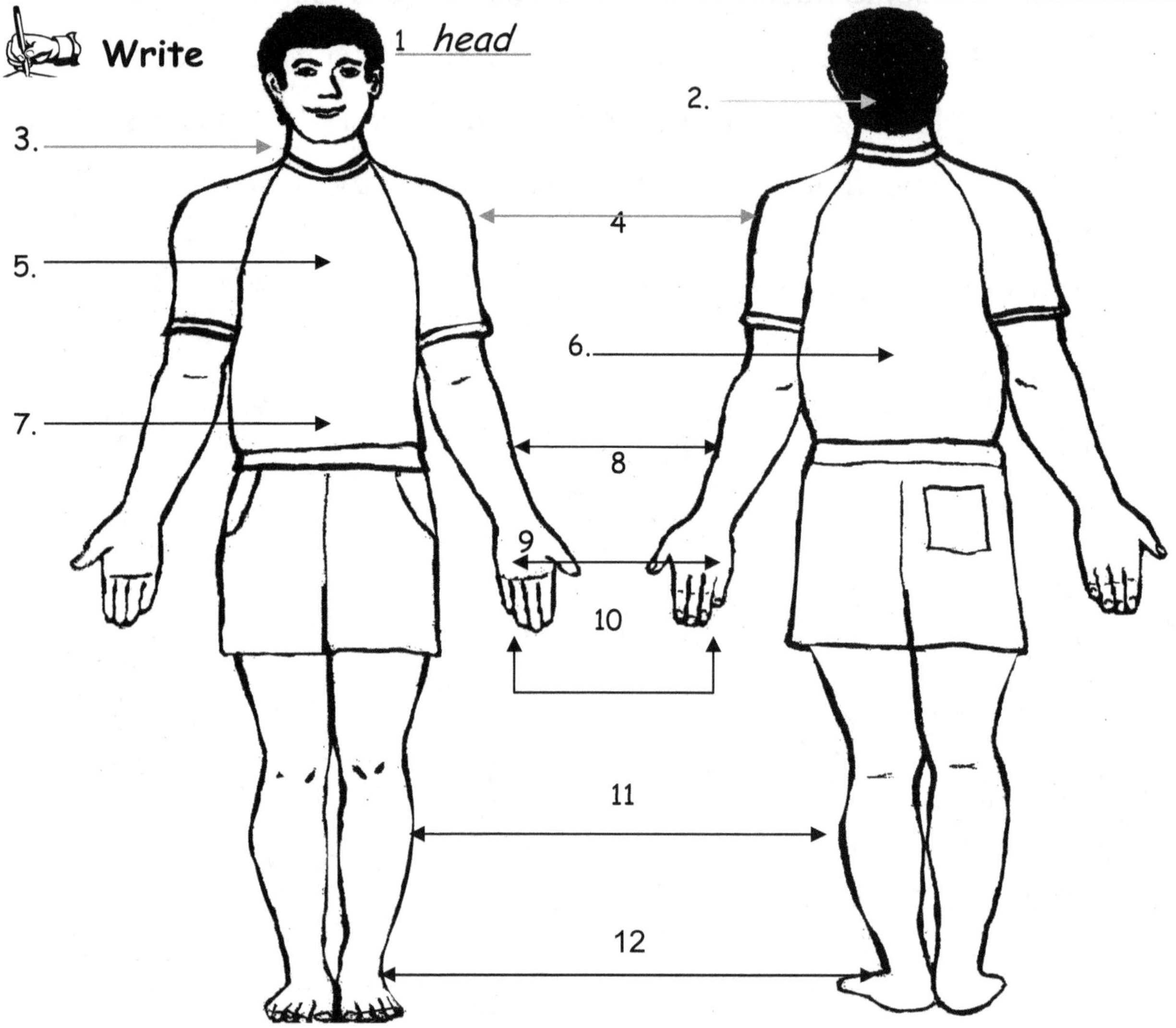

1 _head_
2.
3.
4.
5.
6.
7.
8.
9.
10.
11.
12.

| 13. knee | 14. ankle | 15. toes | 16. knuckles | 17. wrist | 18. elbow |

✏️ **Write**

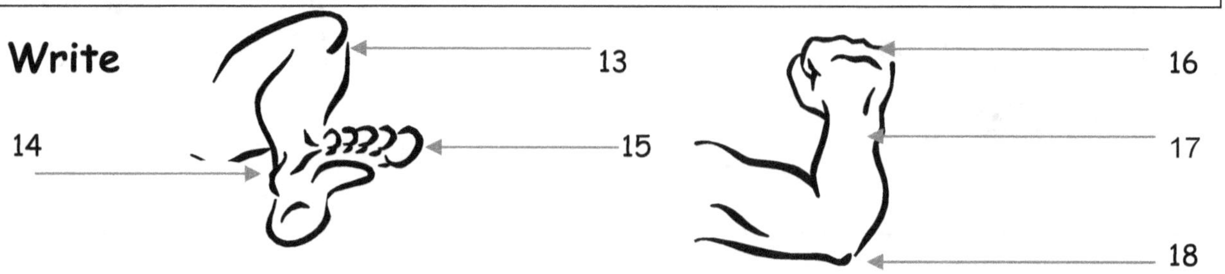

13
14
15
16
17
18

🖍️ Find and highlight eight body words.

m	h	e	a	d	r	k	n	e	e	s	x	f	e	e	t	a
b	a	c	k	o	l	a	a	s	c	h	e	s	t	h	m	r
s	p	s	t	o	m	a	c	h	r	h	l	e	g	s	w	m

English Language Skills - Level 1

66 🎧 **Listen** and **read** the story about Kamil.

My name is Kamil. I don't feel well today. I have a headache and a sore throat. I also have a bad cough and a runny nose. I feel hot and I don't want to eat anything. I think I have the flu. I think I should stay home today so I don't give the symptoms to other people.

I will go back to bed now but I think I should go to the doctor this afternoon.

A symptom is a feeling or problem that shows you are sick.

 Highlight all Kamil's symptoms.

1. What kind of sickness does Kamil have ? _____

2. What does Kamil think he should do? _____

Symptoms

67 🎧 **Listen** and **read** the symptoms.

| 1. headache | 2. back pain | 3. rash | 4. asthma |
| 5. fever | 6. sore throat | 7. stomach ache |

 Write

 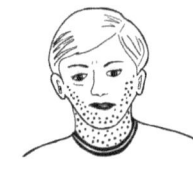 

1. _ _ _ _ _ _ _ _   2. _ _ _ _ _ _ _ _   3. _ _ _ _   4. _ _ _ _ _ _

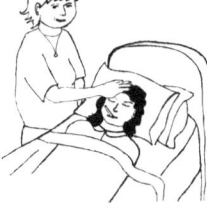  

5. _ _ _ _ _   6. _ _ _ _ _ _ _ _ _ _   7. _ _ _ _ _ _ _ _ _ _ _

Medical checkups

 **Listen**

| 1. x-ray | 2. blood pressure check | 3. blood test |
| 4. breathing check | 5. throat examination | 6. temperature check |

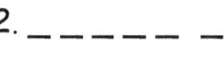 Write

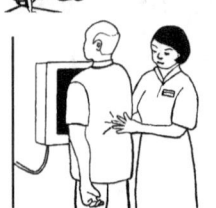    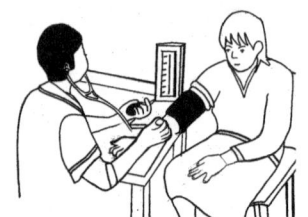   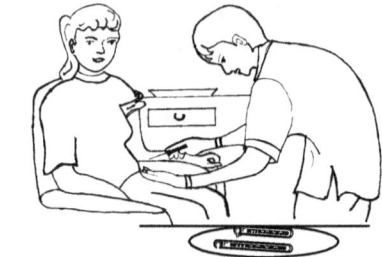

1. _ - _ _ _   2. _ _ _ _ _ _ _ _ _ _ _ _ _ _ _   3. _ _ _ _ _ _ _ _ _ _

   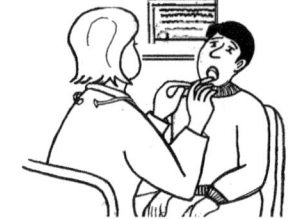   

4. _ _ _ _ _ _ _ _ _ _ _ _ _ _ _   5. _ _ _ _ _ _ _ _   6. _ _ _ _ _ _ _ _ _ _
_ _ _ _ _ _ _ _ _ _ _   _ _ _ _ _

 Listen. Kamil visits his doctor.

Doctor: Hello Kamil. What seems to be the problem?
Kamil: I don't feel well, doctor. I think it's the flu.
Doctor: What are your symptoms?
Kamil: I have a cough and a runny nose. I feel hot and I don't want to eat anything. I have a headache and a sore throat.
Doctor: Mm. How long have you had these symptoms?
Kamil: For two days.
Doctor: I'll give you a prescription for medicine to ease the symptoms. But first I'll check your throat anc' breathing and temperature. Open your mouth please and say 'Ah'.
Kamil: Ah.

What will the doctor check for Kamil?

_____   _____   _____

Saying you don't understand

✏️ Write the words under the pictures.

| rash | washing detergent | products | itchy |

a._____   b._____   c._____   d._____

🎧 70 Listen to Natasha talking to her doctor.

Doctor: Hello Natasha. How can I help you today?
Natasha: I'm worried about this rash on my arms doctor. It's very itchy.
Doctor: Mm, I see. How long have you had it?
Natasha: A few weeks I think.
Doctor: Mm. It may be an allergy to washing detergent. Have you used any new products lately?
Natasha: I'm sorry, doctor. I don't understand. Can you say it again please? And can you write the name of the problem for me?
Doctor: Yes, of course. I said allergy. It means something will make you sick when you eat it, or touch it. I will write it so you can check your dictionary.

1. What is Natasha worried about? _____
2. What does the doctor think may be the problem? _____
3. What did Natasha say when she did not understand?
_____

Checking a dictionary

When we check a dictionary, we need to know alphabetical order.

a b c d e f g h i j k l m n o p q r s t u v w x y z

✏️ Write the words in alphabetical order:

<u>a</u>llergy   <u>t</u>ouch   <u>i</u>tchy   <u>r</u>ash   <u>d</u>etergent

1. _____
2. _____
3. _____
4. _____
5. _____

English Language Skills - Level 1   63   © Boyer Educational Resources

Reading medicine labels

1. tablets   2. drops   3. medicine
4. ointment   5. capsules

Write

1. _____   2. _____   3. _____

4. _____   5. _____

Read the labels.   Write the answers.

1. When should you take a tablet? _____

2. Where should you put the drops? _____

3. How many times a day should you have cough medicine? _____

4. How many times a day should you use the ointment? _____

5. How many capsules should you have in one day? _____

Words and sounds

Listen.
One word has a different sound. Circle the different word.

p<u>ai</u>n   <u>a</u>che   t<u>a</u>ke   b<u>e</u>d   s<u>ay</u>   p<u>ay</u>   d<u>ay</u>

At the pharmacy or chemist

Listen.

Shop Assistant: Can I help you?
Customer: Yes. I need some cough medicine.
Shop Assistant: OK. This medicine is good. It's for children and adults.
Customer: Oh good. Everyone in the family has a cough.
Shop Assistant: Well, this will help. Take 10 ml in the morning and at bed time.
Customer: OK. Thank you.
Shop Assistant: You can pay at the front counter.
Customer: OK. Thanks.

ml = millilitre

1. What does the customer need? _____
2. Who has a cough? _____
3. Where can the customer pay? _____
4. Show how much medicine the customer should put in the medicine cup at bed time. →

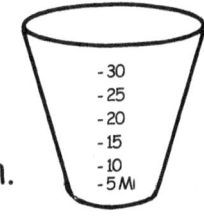

 Practise the conversation with another person.

 Write the words to make sentences.

1. headache have a I
2. has sore throat He a
3. have a I rash
4. one Take tablet with meals.
5. and at bedtime Take 10 ml in the morning
6. daily Apply ointment to rash three times.

Symptoms	Medicine Labels
1.	4.
2.	5.
3.	6.

Staying healthy

73 Listen to the names for food.

| chicken | fish | bread | red meat | cheese |
| soup | noodles | eggs | rice | fruit | vegetables |

Write words below the correct pictures.

1 _fish_   2 _____   3 _____   4 _____

5 _____   6 _____   7 _____   8 _____   9 _____

10 _____   11 _____

74 Listen to Paul talking about what he eats.

Hello, I'm Paul. I'm busy every morning so I only have coffee for breakfast. I usually get hungry at 10 o'clock so I have chocolate or some sweet biscuits. For lunch I have a sandwich with cheese or meat. For dinner I like sausages and chips.
I don't like vegetables or fruit but I love ice cream.
I always have ice cream before I go to bed.

English Language Skills - Level 1

✍ Write answers about Paul.

1. What does Paul have for breakfast? _____

2. What does Paul eat for lunch? _____

3. What does Paul eat for dinner? _____

4. Does Paul eat healthy food? _____

✍ Put a tick ☑ to answer the questions about you.

	Yes, I do.	No, I don't
Do you drink water every day?	☐	☐
Do you eat vegetables every day?	☐	☐
Do you eat fruit every day?	☐	☐

What other food do you eat every day?
_____

Words and sounds

[75 👂] Listen.
One word has a different vowel sound. ⓒircle the different word.

noodles   lunch   soup   fruit   food

Emergency services

| Police | Fire | Ambulance |

✍ Write the emergency service

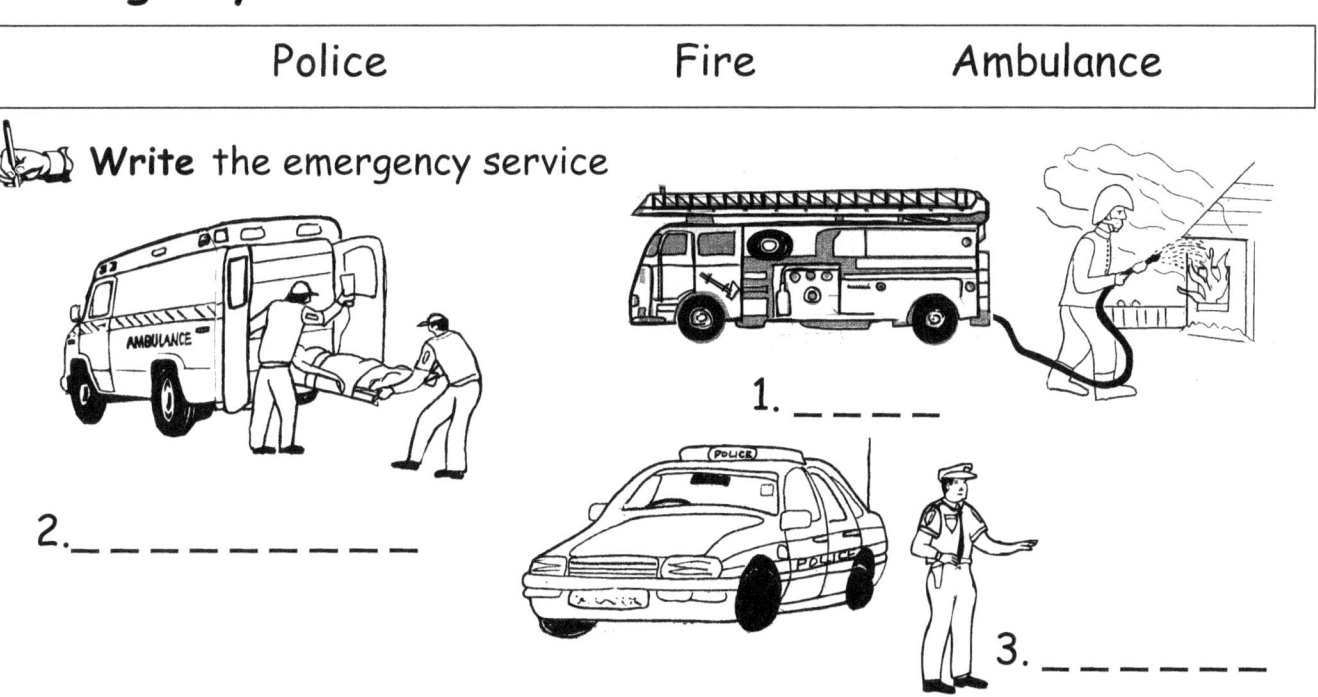

1. _ _ _ _ _

2. _ _ _ _ _ _ _ _

3. _ _ _ _ _ _

English Language Skills - Level 1

Emergency calls

76 **Listen**

Write: Ambulance, Fire or Police.

1. I think my son ate some rat poison!

1. _____

2. Someone took my car from my garage!

2. _____

3. There is a fire in a shop.

3. _____

77 Listen to the people making emergency calls

Write the address.

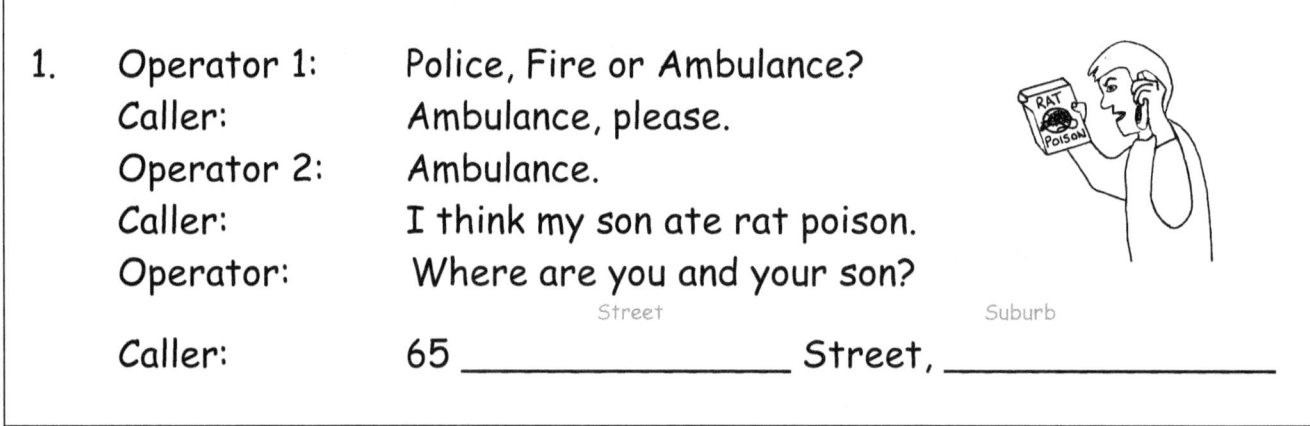

1. Operator 1: Police, Fire or Ambulance?
   Caller: Ambulance, please.
   Operator 2: Ambulance.
   Caller: I think my son ate rat poison.
   Operator: Where are you and your son?
   Caller: 65 _____ Street, _____
                                 Street   Suburb

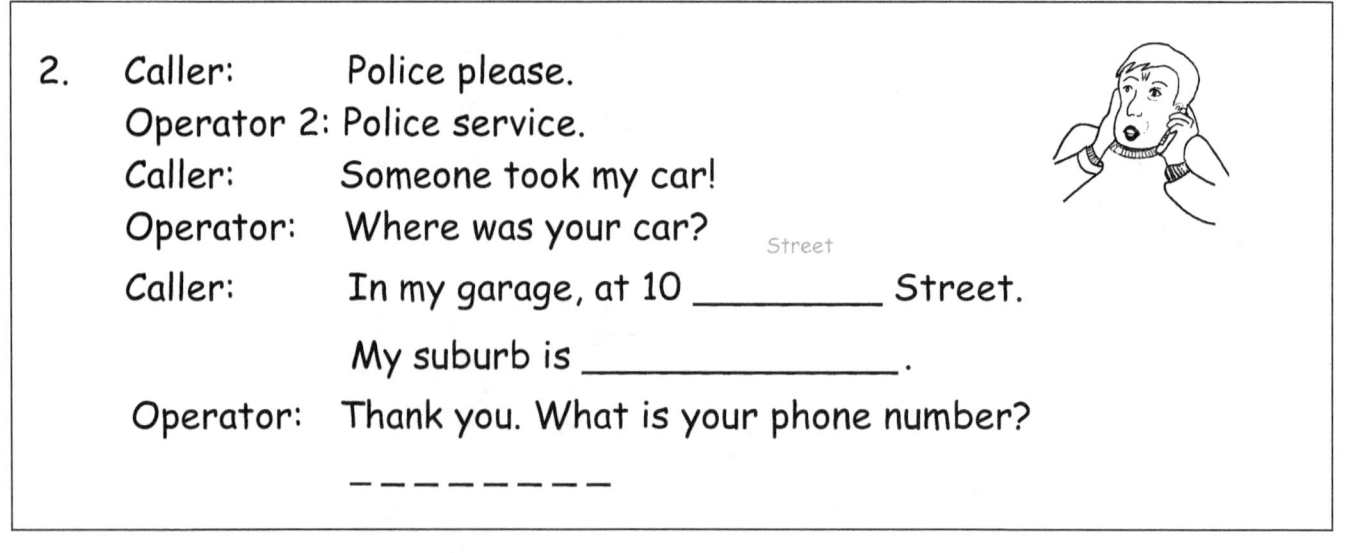

2. Caller: Police please.
   Operator 2: Police service.
   Caller: Someone took my car!
   Operator: Where was your car?
   Caller: In my garage, at 10 _____ Street.
   My suburb is _____.
   Operator: Thank you. What is your phone number?
   _ _ _ _ _ _ _ _

3. Caller: Fire please.
    Operator 2: Fire service.
    Caller: There is a fire in a shop.
    Operator: Where is the shop?
    Caller: It's _____ Street,
                    Number   Street
                 The suburb is _____.

Practise the emergency calls.

What phone number do you call for Police, Ambulance and Fire? __ __ __

What can you do now?

Put a tick ☑ next to things you can do.

1. I can read, write and say some parts of the body. ☐

2. I can say the names of some symptoms. ☐

3. I can say the names of some medical checks. ☐

4. I can write words in alphabetical order. ☐

5. I can read some medicine labels. ☐

6. I know what to say when I don't understand. ☐

7. I can write the names of some food. ☐

8. I can say the names of emergency services. ☐

Unit 6 - Shopping and services

This is Yasmin. She is shopping for food and other things today. This is her shopping list. →

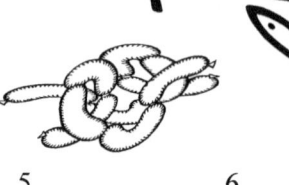

magazine
envelopes
sun screen
sausages
paintbrush
bread rolls

Write the things on the shopping list.

1 _____ 2 _____ 3 _____ 4 _____ 5 _____ 6 _____

Where can she buy the things on her list?
Write the things she can buy in each shop.

_____ _____ _____ _____ _____

What <u>other</u> things can you buy in these shops? Write a list for each shop.

How many?

When we talk about **one** thing we say '**a**'.

Can I have <u>a</u> bread roll please?

When we don't say how many things we want, we use '**some**'.

Can I have <u>some</u> bread rolls please?

Write the words that Yasmin says in the sentences.

| some bread rolls | a magazine | some envelopes |
| a bottle of sun screen | some sausages | a paint brush |

1. At the butcher she says: Can I have _____ please.
2. At the pharmacy she says: Can I have _____ please.

3. At the hardware store she says: Can I have _____ please.

4. At the newsagency she says: Can I have _____
   and _____ please.

5. At the bakery she says: Can I have _____ please.

Asking for things

Listen to a customer ask for thinks at a bakery. He says, 'I would like …' or 'I'd like…' when he asks for something.

[78] Listen to a customer ask for things at the bakery.

Customer: I'd like some small bread rolls please?
Assistant: How many would you like?
Customer: Mm. Ten please. And I'd like some chocolate muffins.
Assistant: How many would you like?
Customer: Six, please.
Assistant: OK. We have a special on donuts today. Buy six, get six free.
Customer: Oh that's a good special. Yes, I'd like some donuts, please.

Highlight where the customer says: **I'd like**…

Practise the conversation with another person.

Ask for different things.

  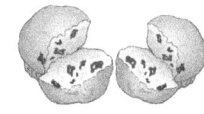  

chocolate slice   small apple pies   fruit buns   cup cakes   a salad roll

Offering food and drinks

Yasmin has some friends at her house for afternoon tea. She says, Would you like...?

 **Listen** to Yasmin offer food and drinks.

Yasmin:	Would you like tea or coffee, Jean?
Jean:	Coffee, please.
Yasmin:	And would you like a donut or a muffin?
Jean:	Mm. The muffins smell good. I'd like a muffin, please.

Highlight the words Yasmin says to offer food and drinks. Practise the conversation with another person.

Shopping in the supermarket

Some people shop for food and other things at the supermarket.

Listen to the supermarket words

| checkout counter | trolley | receipt | customer |
| groceries | aisle | shelves | shopping basket | shopping bag |

Write words with the correct pictures.

a. _____   b. ___*receipt*___   c. _____

d. _____   e. _____   f. _____

g. _____   h. _____   i. _____

English Language Skills - Level 1

Asking where

Yasmin can't find things in the supermarket.

She asks: Excuse me, where is the soap?

 Listen to Yasmin asking where groceries are in the supermarket.

Yasmin:	Excuse me, where is the soap?
Shop Assistant:	It's in aisle one, on the left.
Yasmin:	Thank you, and where is the ice-cream?
Shop Assistant:	It's in aisle four, on the left.
Yasmin:	And where is the dog food?
Shop Assistant:	It's in aisle three, on the right.
Yasmin:	Thank you very much.

 Write the grocery name in the aisle where Yasmin can find it.

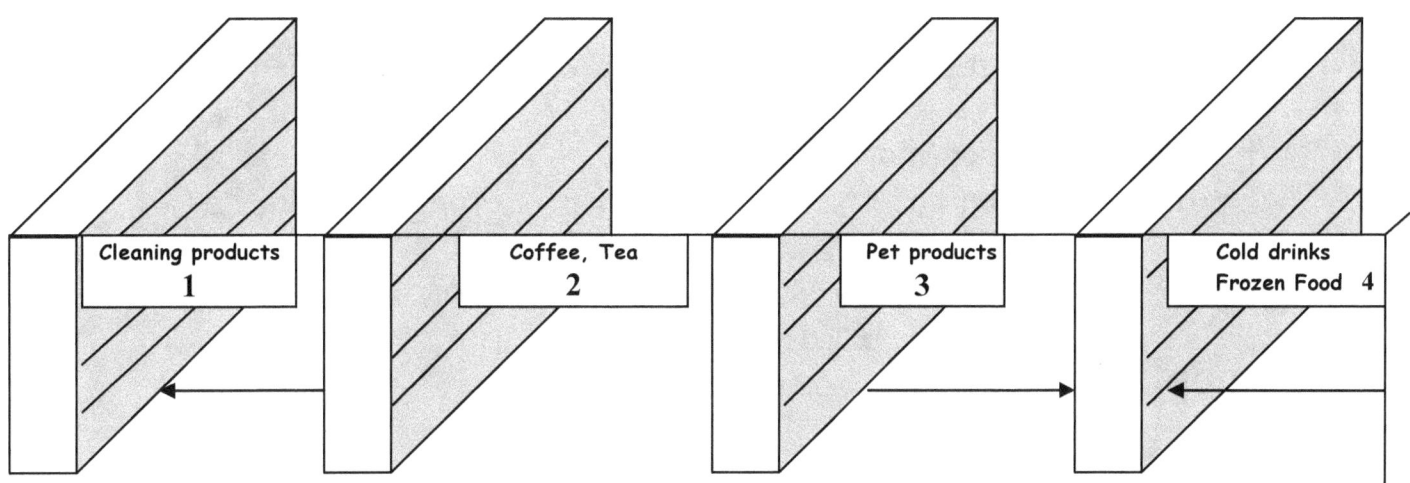

 Practise the conversation with another person. Ask for different things.

milk   cat food   tea   shampoo   apple juice

Groceries

82 Listen. We talk about groceries with different words.

| cans | jars | bottles | bags |
| cartons | tubes | boxes | a piece |

Write the words below the correct picture.

a. _____   b. _____   c. *bottles*   d. _____

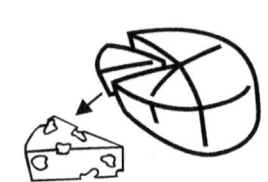

e. _____   f. _____   g. _____   h. _____

How many?

- When we talk about **one** thing we say 'a': **a carton** of milk
- When we say **two or more** things, we put 's' at the end of the thing: **two cartons** of milk
- We can say **some**: **some milk**

A shopping list

Yasmin looks in her cupboard and sees she needs some things.

Write. She needs:

1. a _____ of olives
2. a _____ of olive oil
3. a _____ of cheese
4. a _____ of toothpaste

5. a _____ of soup
6. a _____ of nuts
7. a _____ of eggs

What is in the fridge? Look at the food in the fridge.
Close your book and write a list of the things in the fridge.

83 **Listen** to the questions and answers.

Where are the sausages?	They are **above** the chicken.
Where is the cream?	It is **next to** the chicken.
Where is the jam?	It is **below** the chicken.
Where is the cheese?	It is **between** the lettuce and the lemons.

 Write: above, next to, below or **between**

1. Where are the bananas?   They are _____ the cheese.
2. Where are the apples?   They are _____ the eggs and the pineapple.
3. Where is the honey?   It is _____ the jam.
4. Where is the pineapple?   It is _____

English Language Skills - Level 1

Garage Sale

Kim wants to sell some things. Other people want to buy some things.

What can you see for sale?
Write the names of five things you want to buy.

 Write how much you will pay.

_____   _____
_____   _____
_____   _____
_____   _____
_____   _____

How much?

When we ask about **one** thing, we say: How much **is** the lamp?

When we ask about **two or more** things, we say: How much **are** the shoes?

Practise with another person.
Say: How much is…?
How much are…?

Buying lunch

Read the prices and write how much the customer will pay.

 Listen to a customer asking for things.

Conversation 1

Words and sounds

86 🎧 Listen.
One word has a different vowel sound. Circle the different word.

l<u>i</u>ke   p<u>ie</u>   l<u>i</u>st   <u>ai</u>sle   b<u>uy</u>   b<u>i</u>ke

Matilda's story

87 🎧 Listen and read Matilda's story.

Hello. I'm Matilda and I love shopping. Yesterday I bought some things for my house because they were on special. I bought a new lamp and a blender and some bowls.

But now I have a problem. When I plugged in the blender it didn't work. It is broken. I will go back to the shop today and talk to the shop assistant. I will say I'd like a new blender.

bought = did buy

1. What did Matilda buy yesterday?

_____ _____ _____

2. What happened when Matilda plugged in the blender?

2. It _____

3. What will Matilda do?

3. She _____

4. What will Matilda say to the shop assistant?

4. _____

88 🎧 **Listen** to Matilda's conversation with the shop assistant.

Shop Assistant: Hello. Can I help you?
Matilda: Yes. I bought this blender here yesterday but it is broken.
Shop Assistant: I see. Do you have your receipt?
Matilda: Yes. Here it is.
Shop Assistant: Good. Would you like your money back or a new blender?
Matilda: Oh, I'd like a new blender please.
Shop Assistant: OK. I'll get one for you.
Matilda: Thank you.

Practise the conversation with another person. Ask to change other things

lamp   hairdryer   kettle   vacuum cleaner

Words and sounds

89 🎧 **Listen**.

One word has a different vowel sound. Circle the different word.

c<u>oa</u>t   b<u>o</u>x   s<u>o</u>   g<u>o</u>   n<u>o</u>

What can you do now?

Put a tick ☑ next to things you can do.

1. I can read, write and say some shopping words. ☐
2. I can ask for things in a shop. ☐
3. I can say how many I want. ☐
4. I can offer food and drink. ☐
5. I can ask where something is in a supermarket. ☐
6. I can ask: How much is that? ☐
7. I can ask to change something in a shop. ☐

Unit 7 - Going places

 Listen to transport words.

| train → bicycle | bus | plane | taxi |
| tram | on foot | car | motorbike | boat |

✎ Write the words

1. by _____ 2. by _____ 3. ___ _____

4. by _____ 5. by _____ 6. by _____

7. by _____ 8. by _____ 9. by _____

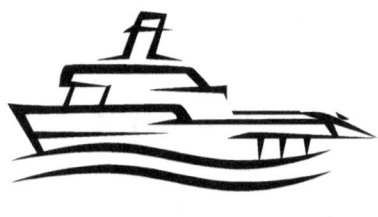

10. by _____

 Find and highlight the transport words.

x	o	t	r	a	i	n	b	a	r	m	p	r	t	z	b	o	a	t
p	l	y	r	w	z	q	u	b	i	c	y	c	l	e	p	r	t	z
q	u	o	t	a	x	i	p	r	m	z	c	z	t	r	q	u	o	
b	u	s	p	r	t	z	a	b	c	g	h	i	p	l	a	n	e	x
f	a	r	n	q	u	o	c	a	r	p	r	t	z	b	a	r	n	b
t	r	a	m	p	r	t	z	o	r	i	n	g	e	q	u	o	i	s
a	b	c	d	e	f	g	h	m	o	t	o	r	b	i	k	e	m	i
o	n		f	o	o	t	c	z	q	u	o	s	p	p	r	t	z	o

 Write about you.

How do you come to your English class?   I come to class _____

How do you go to the shopping centre?   _____

How do you go to the city?   _____

Places in the town and city

 Listen to the names of places

| post office | school | swimming pool | hospital |
| train station | library | gym | cinema | bank |

Places

 Write the place names

1. Where do people post letters? _____ _____
2. Where do people swim? _____ _____
3. Where do students study? _____
4. Where do people put money? _____
5. Where do people watch movies? _____
6. Where do people go to borrow books? _____
7. Where do people go when they are sick? _____
8. Where do people go to catch a train? _____ _____
9. Where do people go to exercise? _____

Adam's story

92 **Listen** and read Adam's story. Highlight the places.

Every day Adam walks to the park with his dog.
He goes to the library on Thursday to borrow books.
It is near his house so he walks there. On Friday he goes to
the post office. He goes by bus because it is far from his house.
Every week he goes by car to the cinema with his friend to watch a movie.

1. When does Adam go to the library? _____
2. How does he go there? _____
3. Where does Adam go on Friday? _____
4. How does he go there? _____
5. When does Adam go to the cinema? _____
6. How does he go there? _____

✍ Write a sentence about Adam next to each picture.

_____

_____

_____

_____

✍ Write some sentences about where **you** go.

I go _____

_____

_____

_____

93 👂 **Listen** to the words about train travel.

| ticket | timetable | platform |
| ticket office | ticket gate | ticket slot |

✍ Write the word below the pictures.

a. _____ b. _____ c. _____

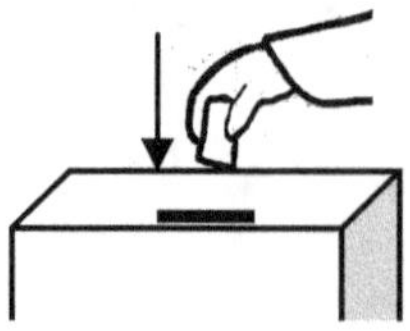

d. _____ e. _____ f. _____

English Language Skills - Level 1

Buying a train ticket

Listen to Adam telling his friend, Joel, how to go by train to the city.

First, read the timetable for the train time and the platform number.
Buy a ticket from the ticket office.
Say, 'I'd like a return ticket to the city please.'

Go to the ticket gate and put the ticket into the slot.
The gate will open. Go through the gate and take the ticket with you.
Go to the platform and wait for the train. Keep the ticket with you on the train.

Write

1. What should Joel do first?
   _____

2. What should Joel say at the ticket office?
   _____

3. What should Joel do at the ticket gate?
   _____

4. What should Joel do with the ticket on the train?
   _____

Read the train timetable

Next train to:	am	am	am	pm
Westmead	9.15	10.15	11.15	12.15
Parramatta	9.18	10.18	11.18	12.18
Strathfield	9.30	10.30	11.30	12.30
Redfern	9.40	10.40		12.40
Central	9.44	10.44	11.42	12.44

Joel gets on the train at Westmead at 10.15 in the morning.

Write

What time will Joel arrive at Central? _____

How long will Joel be on the train? _____

What time is the next train from Westmead to Central? _____

Write the correct sentence for each picture.

Go to the ticket gate and put the ticket into the slot.
Go to the platform and wait for the train.
First, read the timetable for the train time and the platform number.
Go through the gate and take the ticket with you.
Buy a ticket from the ticket office.

1
Trains to:	Depart at:	Platform
City Central	11.30 am	1
Katoomba	11.45	2
Parramatta	12.30	3

2

_____

_____

3

4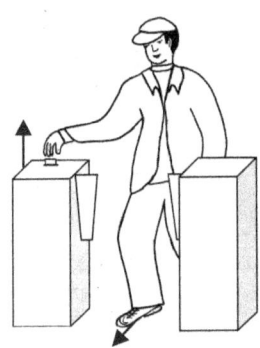

_____

_____

5. _____

_____

Read about Adam's suburb

 My suburb is not busy. There is a park and a library near my house but the post office and shopping centre are far from my house.

 Write sentences about your suburb:

My suburb is _____. There is a _____ near my house but _____ and _____ are far from my house.

Reading a map - Find these places on the map.

Key:

1. ✉ Post Office
2. Ⓗ Hospital
3. 🍽 Restaurant
4. 🌳 Park
5. 🚌 Bus stop
6. ⊢▬⊣ Railway Station
7. 📖 Library
8.) Public phone
9. Ⓟ Car Park
10. 🚓 Police station
11. 🏘 Houses

95 👂 Listen to Conversation 1.   ✍ Draw a line to show the direction.

Excuse me, where is the post office?
It's in North Street.
Go along Main Street and turn right at North Street.
Thank you.

96 👂 Listen to Conversation 2.

Excuse me, where is the library?
It's in High Street.
Go along Main Street and turn left at High Street.
Thank you.

Excuse me, where is the hospital?

_____

_____   ✍ Write the directions.

🗣 Practise.

This year

Read what some students learnt this year.

1. This year I learnt to write information on a form.

2. This year I learnt about syllables in words.

3. This year I learnt to read words on medicine labels.

4. This year I learnt to ask for things in a shop.

What about **you**? Write.

This year I learnt _____

_____

Look at the poster about what students learnt this year.

What words and sentences did you learn this year?

 Write words and sentences you learnt on a poster.

Show your poster to other students.

Next year

Read what some students want to do next year.
They are talking about their goals.

1. Next year I want to get a part-time job. First, I will study more English.

2. Next year I want to study hairdressing. First, I will practise more English.

3. Next year I want to travel to different places. First, I will save some money.

What about **you**?   Write.

Next year I want to _____

First, I will _____

What can you do now?

Put a tick ☑ next to things you can do.

1. I can read and say the names of types of transport. ☐

2. I can read and say the names of places in towns and cities. ☐

3. I can read a short story and answer questions. ☐

4. I can write sentences about a picture. ☐

5. I can ask for directions. ☐

6. I can buy a train ticket. ☐

7. I can talk about my goals. ☐

Answers
Unit 1 English class, page 5

Names of people	Names of places
Tejinder	India
Ana	Chile
Kim	China
Jo	Egypt
Mai	
Jack	

page 5   1. My name is Kim.   2. I come from China.

page 6
1. Ali   1. Turkey
2. Natasha   2. Russia
3. David   3. Australia

My first name is <u>Eva</u>.
My surname is <u>Milton</u>.
My address is <u>221 Home Street</u>.
My suburb is <u>Lapstone</u>.
My postcode is <u>2773</u>

1. First name: Eva	2. Surname: Milton
3. Address: 221 Home Street	
4. Suburb: Lapstone	
5. Postcode: 2773	

Syllables, page 12

door	1	scissors	2	name	1	pencil	2
teacher	2	desk	1	surname	2	telephone	3
student	2	classroom	2	word	1	sentence	2
syllable	3	book	1	ruler	2	story	2

Counting things, page 13
1. watche**s** (two things)
2. book**s** (two things)
3. pencil (one thing)
4. student (one thing)
5. glasse**s** (two things)

Signs, page 14
a. No parking
b. Library
c. Canteen
d. Exit
e. Lost property
f. No smoking
g. Toilet
h. Enquiries

Saying hello and goodbye, page 15

Len: Hello Sue. <u>How</u> are you? [1.]
Sue: Really well <u>thanks</u>. How was your weekend? [2.]
Len: Really <u>good</u>, thank you. <u>How</u> was your weekend? [3.] [4.]
Sue: It was great.
Len: That's good.
Sue: Well I'd better <u>go</u>. See you later. [5.]
Len: Yes. <u>Bye</u> now. [6.]

Asking for directions, page 16 - 17

3. Turn <u>left</u> at the corner.   4. Turn <u>right</u> at the corner.   5. Turn <u>left</u> at the corner
   It is on the <u>left</u>.   It is on the <u>right</u>.   and it is on the <u>right</u>.

Words and sounds – page 17   pl<u>ea</u>se   m<u>e</u>   (t<u>e</u>n)   thr<u>ee</u>   s<u>ee</u>

Unit 2 Talking about people - Giving information, page 22

2. I come from Australia.
3. I like dogs.
4. I have a brother.
5. I am a student.

Rona Green, page 24

My name is Rona Green.
I have two children. My daughter, Rita, is ten years old.
My son, Tim, is two years old. I speak Spanish
because I come from Chile, in South America.

I teach Spanish to other people every Monday morning.
On Monday I take my son, Tim, to Kindy Childcare Centre.
He is happy because he likes playing with the other children.

A form, page 24

Kindy Childcare Centre Form	
Family name: Green	Name of mother: Rona Name of child: Tim
Address: 268 King Road Suburb: Hopetown	Postcode: 2999

Name and address, page 25

Giving information about other people, page 26

1. <u>This is</u> my husband, David. 2. <u>He is</u> a teacher.

3. <u>This is</u> my friend, Rita.   <u>She is</u> from South America.

4. <u>This is</u> my reading book.   <u>It is</u> interesting.

page 27

1. This is Rita. <u>She</u> has short, straight black hair.
2. This is Susan. <u>She</u> has long, straight blonde hair.
3. This is Jo. <u>He</u> has short, curly black hair.
4. This is Omar. <u>He</u> has dark skin and a big smile. He is bald.
5. This is Bella. <u>She</u> has long, wavy blonde hair.
6. This is Boris. <u>He</u> has fair skin and short, blonde hair.
7. This is Ali. <u>He</u> has a moustache. <u>He</u> is wearing a cap.
8. This is Yasmin. <u>She</u> is wearing a scarf.
9. This is Tejinder. <u>He</u> has a moustache and a beard. <u>He</u> is wearing a turban.
10. This is Mohamed. He has He has a <u>beard</u> and a <u>moustache</u>.
11. This is Rene. She has <u>curly</u> black hair.
12. This is Michelle. She has <u>long, straight</u> black hair.
13. This is Karl. He has curly <u>blonde</u> hair.
14. This is David. H e has <u>short</u>, black hair.

Unit 2 Talking about other people – photographs, page 29

Ann: This is my sister's wedding.
     It is in my garden.

Tim: Really? It looks beautiful.

Ann: Thank you.
     And this is a photo of my friends, Ken and Lin.
     They <u>are</u> from China. They <u>are</u> students in my class.

Tim: They look friendly.

Ann: Yes, they <u>are</u>. And this is a photo of my
     class party. This <u>is</u> my teacher here.

Tim: Yes, I see. And where is this?

Ann: This <u>is</u> my house here.
     And this <u>is</u> my dog.

Words and sounds – page 29   b<u>oo</u>t   sh<u>oe</u>s   (d<u>o</u>g)   tw<u>o</u>   y<u>ou</u>

Asking questions – page 30

1. <u>Who</u> is this?   2. <u>Who</u> is this?   3. <u>Where</u> is this?
4. <u>Who</u> is this?   5. <u>What</u> is this?   6. <u>Who</u> is this?

Talking about other people – page 30

The pronoun for a man is <u>he</u>
The pronoun for a woman is <u>she</u>
The pronoun for <u>more than one</u> person is <u>they</u>
The pronoun for a place is <u>it</u>

Using Pronouns: He, she, they, it – page 31

> **Jane and Mike**
> This is Jane. <u>She</u> is 34 years old and she is a teacher.
> <u>She</u> is married to Mike. <u>He</u> is a mechanic. <u>He</u> likes his job
> because he likes cars.
>
> Jane and Mike have been married for ten years.
> <u>They</u> have two children. <u>They</u> live in a place called Newtown.
> <u>It</u> is a busy place near the city.

Saying English words – syllables – page 32

niece	1	mother	2	women	2
father	2	nephew	2	grandson	2
daughter	2	brother	2	grandfather	3

Syllables and Word Stress

• .   • .   • .   • .
student   garden   father   question

• .   • .   • .   • . .
children   husband   cousin   grandmother

Giving information – Using verbs – page 33

1. My name <u>is</u> David.   2. I <u>come</u> from Australia.
3. I <u>like</u> soccer.
4. I <u>have</u> a son and a daughter   5. I <u>am</u> a teacher.
   I <u>have</u> one brother.

Unit 3 Everyday activities, page 34

My name <u>is</u> Kara. I <u>come</u> from Spain. I <u>have</u> two sons.
I <u>am</u> a nurse in a big hospital. I <u>like</u> computer games.

Write a verb under each picture.
a. <u>cook</u>   b. <u>walk</u>   c. <u>watch</u>   d. <u>drive</u>   e. <u>write</u>
f. <u>sing</u>   g. <u>listen</u>   h. <u>drink</u>   i. <u>shop</u>   j. <u>read</u>

Draw a line under the <u>verb.</u>
1. I <u>walk</u> in the park.
2. I <u>cook</u> my food.
3. I <u>watch</u> TV with my family.
4. I <u>write</u> a letter.
5. I <u>drive</u> to the city.
6. I <u>sing</u> a song.
7. I <u>listen</u> on the telephone.
8. I <u>drink</u> tea in a mug.
9. I <u>read</u> my book.
10. I <u>shop</u> for food and other things.

```
1           w  a  l  k
2              c  o  o  k
3           w  a  t  c  h
4           w  r  i  t  e
5     d  r  i  v  e
6              s  i  n  g
7     l  i  s  t  e  n
8        d  r  i  n  k
9              r  e  a  d
10             s  h  o  p
```

page 35
1. I <u>walk</u> in the park with my friend.
2. I <u>cook</u> food for my friends.
3. I <u>watch</u> a movie on TV with my family.
4. I <u>write</u> emails to my friends.
5. I <u>drive</u> to the city every day.
6. I <u>sing</u> a song when I am happy.
7. I <u>listen</u> to my friend on the phone.
8. I <u>drink</u> water every day.
9. I <u>read</u> my book in bed.
10. I <u>shop</u> for food and other things on Friday.

What can John and Kate do? page 36

John can <u>drive</u> but he can't <u>cook.</u>
Kate can <u>cook</u> and <u>swim</u> but she can't <u>speak Chinese</u>.

What can you do? page 36

a. draw   b. use a computer   c. play a guitar
d. sew   e. ride a bicycle   f. play cards

Talking about activities we like doing, page 37

My name is Rita. I like shopping with my husband, Jack.
I like visiting my friends and talking about our children.
I like driving near my home but I don't like driving in busy places.
I like watching funny movies on TV but I don't like watching sad movies.
I like reading emails from my friends but I don't like writing emails.
I like cooking but I don't like cleaning the kitchen.

page 37 Rita says: I like   **I don't like**

shopping with my husband
visiting my friends
talking about my children
driving near my home   don't like driving in busy places
watching funny movies   don't like watching sad movies
reading emails from my friends   don't like writing emails
cooking   don't like cleaning the kitchen

What do you like doing? page 38

a. swimming b. running c dancing d. drawing
e. sewing f. flying g. cycling h. playing games
i. fishing j. watching sport

Jobs, page 39

1. mechanic 2. chef 3. builder
4. plumber 5. teacher 6. cleaner
7. electrician 8. hairdresser 9. shop assistant

1. A <u>builder</u> builds houses. 6. A <u>cleaner</u> cleans places.
2. A <u>mechanic</u> repairs cars. 7. An <u>electrician</u> repairs electrical things.
3. A <u>chef</u> cooks food. 8. A <u>hairdresser</u> cuts hair.
4. A <u>plumber</u> repairs toilets. 9. A <u>shop assistant</u> sells things.
5. A <u>teacher</u> teaches people.

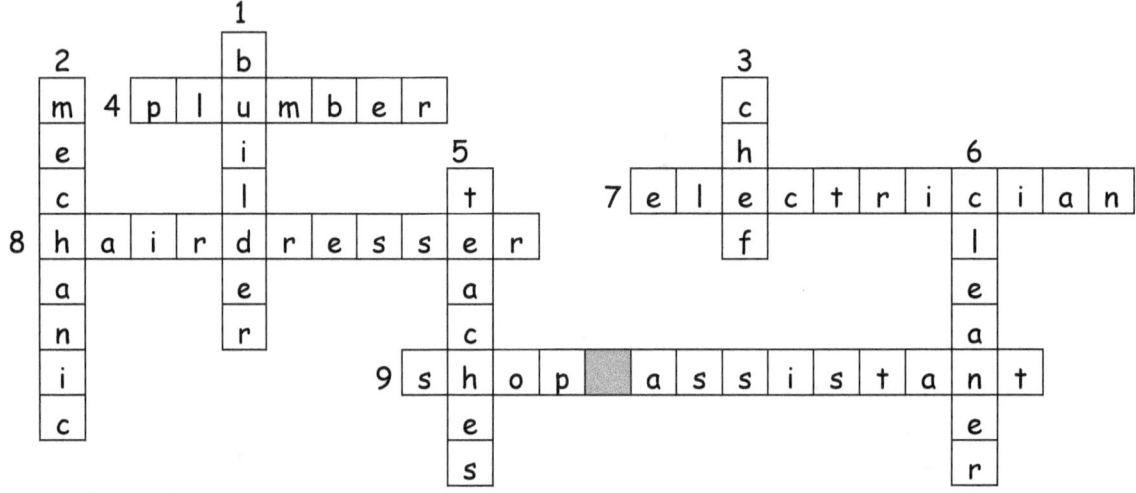

What do people do in their jobs? page 40

1. A builder <u>builds</u> houses.
2. A mechanic <u>repairs</u> cars.
3. A chef <u>cooks</u> food.
4. A plumber <u>repairs</u> toilets and water pipes.
5. A teacher <u>teaches</u> people.
6. A cleaner <u>cleans</u> places.
7. An electrician <u>repairs</u> electrical things.
8. A hairdresser <u>cuts</u> hair.
9. A shop assistant <u>sells</u> things.

Tim, page 40

Tim is a cleaner. He cleans buildings and windows six days each week. He gets up early and has a quick breakfast. Then he drives to the city.

When he is very busy, his sister Jill helps him. Jill washes the windows and Tim sweeps the floors. At the end of a busy day he thanks her very much. He tells her she is a very good sister. She smiles and says he is a good brother too.

page 41
Which word has two syllables? <u>washes</u> has two syllables

English Language Skills - Level 1 © Boyer Educational Resources

page 41

v	s	m	i	l	e	s	h	t	w	x	c	l	e	a	n	s
n	w	u	c	r	o	d	r	i	v	e	s	a	e	c	h	e
s	m	n	g	x	l	h	e	l	p	s	o	d	a	h	a	q
h	a	s	m	n	g	k	a	x	r	p	k	l	t	v	r	t
d	o	e	s	x	t	h	a	n	k	s	g	t	e	l	l	s
w	a	s	h	e	s	g	w	l	e	q	r	l	l	x	m	y

Tim is a cleaner. He clean(s) buildings and windows six days each week.
He get(s) up early and has a quick breakfast. Then he drive(s) to the city.

When he is very busy, his sister Jill help(s) him. Jill wash(es) the windows
and Tim sweep(s) the floors. At the end of a busy day he thank(s) her very
much. He tell(s) her she is a very good sister. She smile(s) and say(s)
he is a good brother too.

Stories about other people, page 42

1. Mai comes from Vietnam.
2. She is twenty-two years old.
3. Now she lives in New Zealand.
4. She is a shop assistant.
5. She works on Friday and Saturday.
6. She likes singing and dancing.
7. She goes to English classes on Monday, Wednesday and Thursday.

What does Mai look like? page 42
Mai has straight, black hair.
She is young.

Words and sounds, page 43   w<u>a</u>tch   (wh<u>a</u>t)   w<u>a</u>sh   d<u>o</u>   sh<u>o</u>p

Unit 4 Talking about time and events, page 44

1. There are 24 <u>hours</u> in a <u>day</u>.
2. There are 7 days in a <u>week</u>.
3. There are 4 weeks in a <u>month</u>.
4. There are 52 weeks in each <u>year</u>.
5. <u>o'clock</u> is used to show the hour in time.
6. <u>Noon</u> means 12 o'clock in the middle of the day.
7. <u>Morning</u> means before noon.
8. <u>Afternoon</u> means after noon.
9. <u>Weekend</u> means Saturday and Sunday.

How many syllables in each word?

Monday <u>2</u> Tuesday <u>2</u> Wednesday <u>2</u> Thursday <u>2</u> Friday <u>2</u> Saturday <u>3</u> Sunday <u>2</u>

Months of the year, page 45

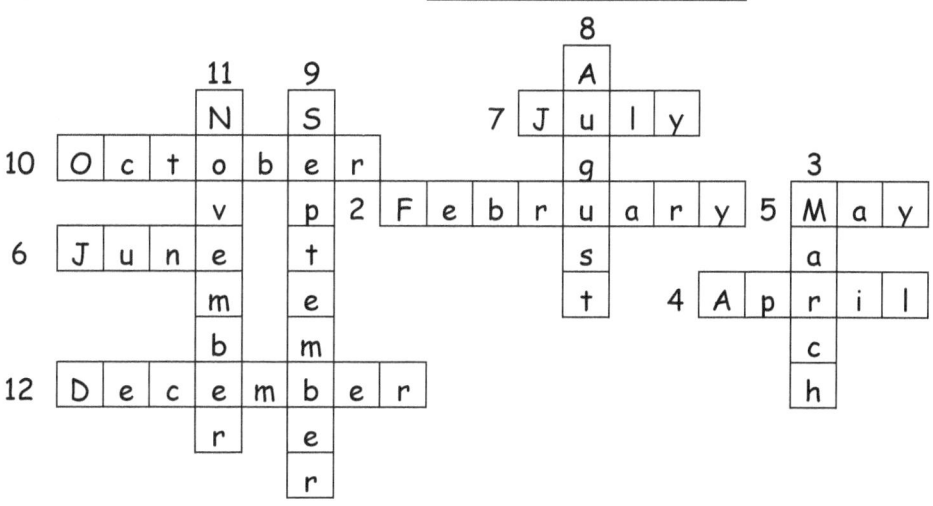

Seasons of the year, page 45

Australia, New Zealand, South America, South Africa (Southern hemisphere)

Summer December January February	**Autumn** March April May
Winter June July August	**Spring** September October November

Europe, USA, UK, etc (Northern hemisphere)

Summer June July August	**Autumn** September October November
Winter December January February	**Spring** March April May

How many syllables are in the name of each month? page 45

January	4	February	4	March	1	April	2
May	1	June	1	July	2	August	2
September	3	October	3	November	3	December	3

Talking about routine, page 47

My name is Jack. I wake up at 6:30 and get up at 6:45.
I have my breakfast at 7 o'clock. I go to work at 9 o'clock.
In the evening, I watch the news and sport on television at 6 o'clock.
I have dinner at 7 o'clock and I go to bed at 10:30 and read a book.
I go to sleep at 11 o'clock.

Boris and Natasha's routine, page 48

My name is Boris and my wife's name is Natasha.
My wife works in a shop and I'm a mechanic.
Every afternoon we walk in the park with our dog.
We always go to English class on Monday night.

We often meet with friends on Friday night. Usually we eat dinner together and sometimes we watch a movie. On Saturday we clean the house and the garden. On Sunday we usually go out somewhere. Sometimes we go for a picnic by the river. Sometimes we go to the beach. We never work on Sunday because it is our day off.

Answers
1. Boris and Natasha go to the park every afternoon.
2. They go to English class Monday night.
3. They meet with friends on Friday night.
4. On Saturday they clean the house and the garden.
5. On Sunday they go out somewhere. They never work on Sunday.

Words and sounds, page 48   wife   like   (did)   night   time   drive

Saying when we do things, page 49

1. I always drink tea in the morning.
2. I often cook Chinese food.
3. I never write emails to my friends.
4. I often drive to the city.
5. I usually listen to music in the car.
6. Sometimes I watch the news on TV.
7. I shop for food and other things once a week.
8. I walk to my English class every day.

Past, present and future time, page 50

past time	present time	future time
yesterday did	now	tomorrow next month
last month last year	at present	next year will

Questions about the past, page 50

1. Did you have fish for breakfast? Yes, I did. ✓ No, I didn't. ☐
2. Did you watch TV last night? Yes, I did. ☐ No, I didn't. ✓
3. Did you walk in the park yesterday? Yes, I did. ☐ No, I didn't. ✓
4. Did you have a busy weekend? Yes, I did. ✓ No, I didn't. ☐

Syllables, page 51

walked [1]   looked [1]   talked [1]
missed [1]   liked [1]   worked [1]
started [2] needed [2]   wanted [2]

Answers, page 51

I lived in Italy.
I started my English class in May.
I talked to my neighbour.
I played ball games.

page 52

a. Yesterday I <u>walked</u> in the park with my friend.
b. Yesterday I <u>cooked</u> food for my friends.
c. Last night I <u>watched</u> a movie on TV with my family.
d. Last night I <u>listened</u> to music.
e. Yesterday I <u>shopped</u> for food and other things.
f. Last week I <u>played</u> cards with my friends.

Mai's weekend, page 52

My name is Mai. Last weekend I <u>visited</u>[1] friends. On Saturday morning we <u>walked</u>[2] to the park and <u>talked</u>[3] for an hour. At lunchtime we <u>cooked</u>[4] a big plate of pancakes and <u>listened</u>[5] to music. In the afternoon we <u>shopped</u>[6] for new clothes at the shopping centre. After dinner we <u>watched</u>[7] a movie and then we <u>played</u>[8] games on the computer.

page 53

1. They <u>walked</u> to the park and <u>talked</u> for an hour.
2. At lunchtime they <u>cooked</u> a big plate of pancakes and <u>listened</u> to music.
3. In the afternoon they <u>shopped</u> for new clothes at the shopping centre.
4. After dinner they <u>watched</u> a movie and then they <u>played</u> games on the computer.

More past tense verbs, page 53

1. Yesterday was hot.
2. I went to the supermarket yesterday.
3. I did my homework last night.
4. I saw a kangaroo last week.
5. Yesterday I bought new shoes.
6. We came to this country last year.

Write a sentence next to each picture, page 53.

a. We came to this country last year.
b. I saw a kangaroo last week.
c. Yesterday I bought new shoes.
d. I went to the supermarket yesterday.
e. I did my homework last night.
f. Yesterday was hot.

Jo's Story, page 54

My name is Jo. When I was a child I lived in Africa on a farm.
When I was sixteen I went to school in the city.
I lived with my aunt and uncle for two years. I went
to school with my cousins and saw many new things.
After school I worked in my uncle's shop for two years.

When I was nineteen I bought a motorbike. On weekends I went to
different places on my motorbike. Sometimes I went to the mountains.
Sometimes I went to the beach.
Now I live in the city and I am a mechanic.

1. He lived in Africa on a farm.
2. He lived with his aunt and uncle for two years.
3. He worked in his uncle's shop,
4. He bought a motorbike.
5. Sometimes he went to the mountains. Sometimes he went to the beach.

Words and sounds, page 54   bought      walk   talk   saw

Past tense verbs, page 55

Present	Past	Present	Past	Present	Past
1. shop	shopped	5. play	played	9. talk	talked
2. is	was	6. see	saw	10. go	went
3. buy	bought	7. come	came	11. walk	walked
4. cook	cooked	8. do	did	12. live	lived

Past tense verbs crossword, page 55

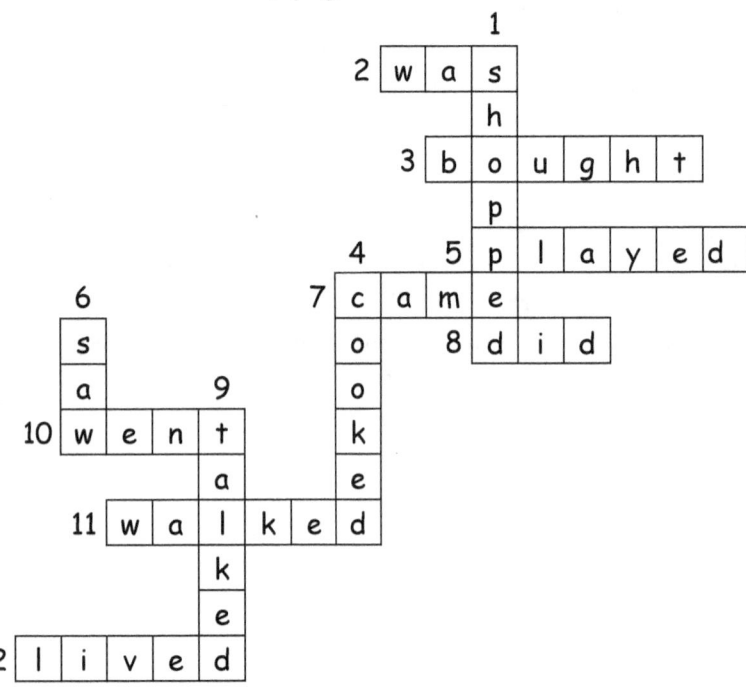

Chinese New Year, page 56

1. Yesterday Kim went shopping.
2. Today she is busy cooking.
3. Tomorrow will be Chinese New Year.
4. Kim will have a big dinner with her family. They will eat fish and vegetables and watch fireworks. They will watch a lion dance.

Special days, page 57

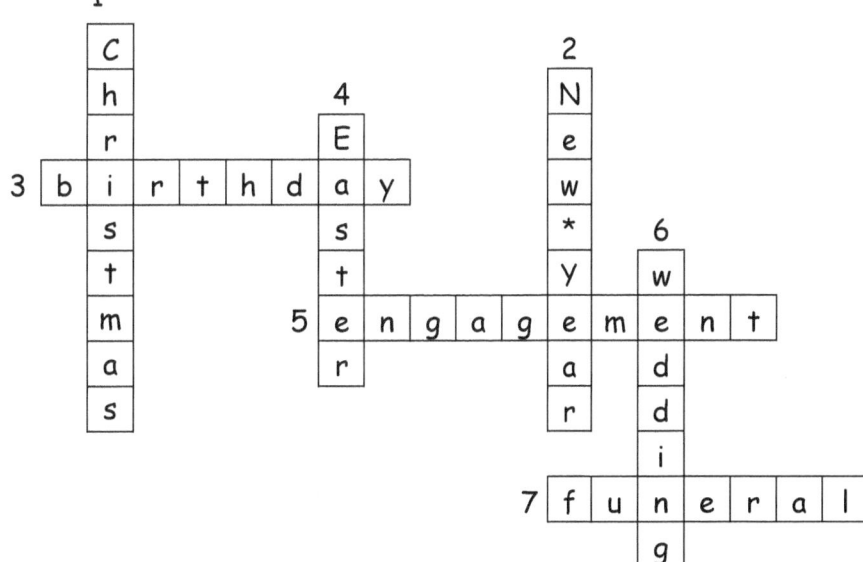

Words and sounds, page 57 n<u>oo</u>n   J<u>u</u>ne   (m<u>o</u>nth)   d<u>o</u>   m<u>oo</u>n

Bob's Story, page 58
My name <u>is</u> Bob. On Saturday we <u>had</u> a barbecue in our garden. I <u>cooked</u> the meat and my wife <u>cooked</u> the vegetables. Many friends <u>came</u> to our house. It <u>was</u> a very good day.

Bella's Story, page 58
My name is Bella. Yesterday <u>was</u> my birthday. I <u>went</u> to the city with my friends. They <u>bought</u> my lunch at a café and then we <u>went</u> to the cinema and watched a movie. It <u>was</u> a very good day.

Our holiday, page 59
Last week we went to our friend's house for a holiday. On Monday we played cards in the afternoon. On Tuesday we walked in the park and saw some ducks. On Wednesday we stayed home and worked in the garden. On Thursday we went for a ride on our bicycles. On Friday we watched a funny movie on TV. On Saturday we had a barbecue in the garden. On Sunday we went home.

a. Monday   b. Thursday   c. Tuesday
d. Wednesday e. Saturday   f. Friday   g. Sunday

Words and sounds, page 59   c<u>ar</u>ds   g<u>ar</u>den   b<u>ar</u>becue   f<u>ar</u>m   p<u>ar</u>k   (h<u>a</u>d)

Unit 5 Health and Safety, page 60

Highlight eight body words:

m	h	e	a	d	r	k	n	e	e	s	x	f	e	e	t	a
b	a	c	k	o	l	a	a	s	c	h	e	s	t	h	m	r
s	p	s	t	o	m	a	c	h	r	h	l	e	g	s	w	m

Kamil, page 61
My name is Kamil. I don't feel well today. I have a headache and a sore throat. I also have a bad cough and a runny nose. I feel hot and I don't want to eat anything. I think I have the flu. I think I should stay home today so I don't give the symptoms to other people.

I will go back to bed now but I think I should go to the doctor this afternoon.

page 61
1. Kamil has the flu.
2. Kamil thinks he should go to the doctor.

Symptoms, page 61
1. headache 2. back pain 3. rash 4. asthma
5. fever   6. sore throat 7. stomach ache

Kamil visits his doctor, page 62
The doctor will check Kamil's: throat, breathing, temperature.
Saying you don't understand, page 63
a. rash   b. itchy   c. products   d. washing detergent
Natasha talking to her doctor, page 63
1. She is worried about her the rash on her arms.
2. It may be an allergy to washing detergent.
3. I'm sorry, doctor. I don't understand. Can you say it again please?
   And can you write the name of the problem for me?
Checking a dictionary, page 63   1. <u>a</u>llergy   2. <u>d</u>etergent   3. <u>i</u>tchy   4. <u>r</u>ash   5. <u>t</u>ouch
Read the labels, page 64
1. with meals   2. Eyes   3. twice (two times) a day   4. three times daily   5. two

Words and sounds, page 64   p<u>ai</u>n   <u>a</u>che   t<u>a</u>ke   (b<u>e</u>d)   s<u>ay</u>   p<u>ay</u>   d<u>ay</u>
At the pharmacy or chemist, page 65
1. cough medicine   2. everyone in the family   3. at the front counter   4. 10ml
Write the words to make sentences, page 65
1. I have a headache.   4. Take one tablet with meals.
2. He has a sore throat.   5. Take 10 ml in the morning and at bed time.
3. I have a rash.   6. Apply ointment to rash three times daily.

Symptoms	Medicine Labels
1. I have a headache.	4. Take one tablet with meals.
2. He has a sore throat.	5. Take 10 ml in the morning and at bed time.
3. I have a rash.	6. Apply ointment to rash three times daily.

Staying healthy, page 66
1. fish   2. bread   3. noodles   4. chicken   5. eggs   6. cheese   7. soup   8. rice
9. red meat   10. fruit   11. vegetables

Answers about Paul, page 67
1. breakfast: coffee
2. lunch: a sandwich with cheese or meat
3. sausages and chips   4. No
Words and sounds, page 67   noodles   (lunch)   soup   fruit   food
Emergency services, page 67
1. Fire   2. Ambulance   3. Police
Emergency calls, page 68
1.. Ambulance   2. Police   3. Fire
Listen to people making emergency calls, page 68 - 69
 1. 65 Long Street, Lapstone.
 2. 10 Short Street, Newtown.
    Phone number: 47 39 1538
 3. 22 Grafton Street, Penrith.

Unit 6 Shopping and services, page 70

1. bread rolls 2. magazine 3. envelopes 4. sun screen 5. sausages 6. paint brush

Pharmacy	Butcher	Bakery	Hardware	Newsagency
sun screen	sausages	bread rolls	paint brush	magazine, envelopes

How many, page 70 - 71

1. At the butcher she says: Can I have <u>some sausages</u> please.
2. At the pharmacy she says: Can I have <u>a bottle of sunscreen</u> please
3. At the hardware store she says: Can I have <u>a paint brush</u> please.
4. At the newsagency she says: Can I have <u>a magazine and some envelopes</u> please.
5. At the bakery she says: Can I have <u>some bread rolls</u> please.

Shopping in the supermarket, page 72

a. trolley   b. receipt   c. checkout counter
d. aisle   e. customer   f. groceries
g. shopping basket   h. shopping bag   i. shelves

Asking where, page 73

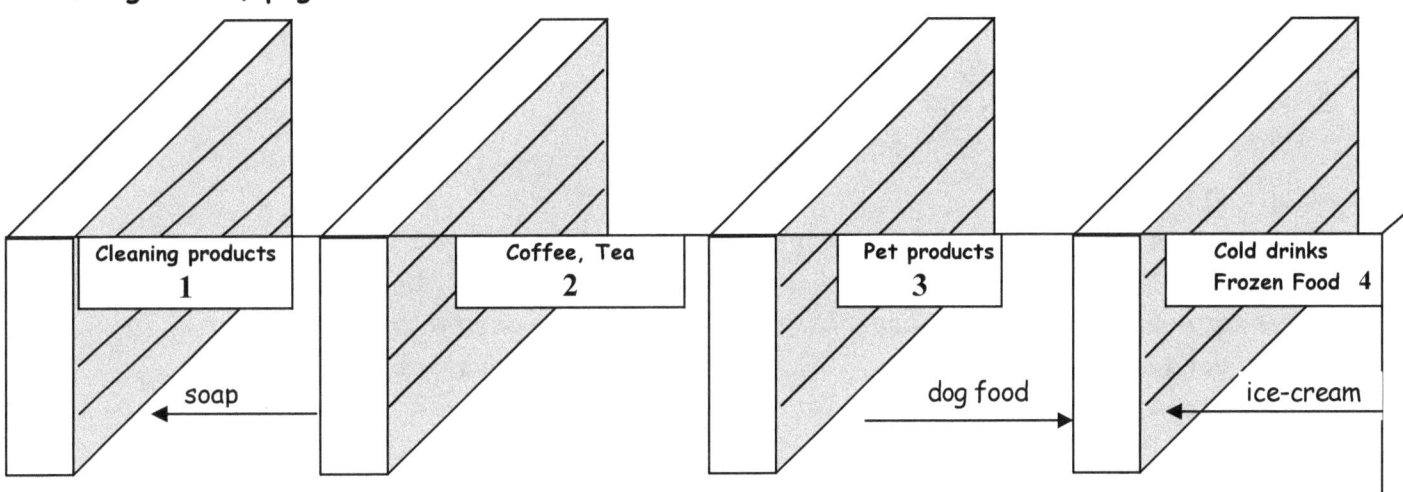

Groceries, page 74

a. tubes   b. cans   c. bottles   d. bags
e. cartons f. jars   g. boxes   h. a piece

A shopping list, page 74

She needs:
1. a <u>jar</u> of olives
2. a <u>bottle</u> of olive oil
3. a <u>piece</u> of cheese
4. a <u>tube</u> of toothpaste
5. a <u>can</u> of soup
6. a <u>bag</u> of nuts
7. a <u>carton</u> of eggs

What is in the fridge, page 75

1. Where are the bananas?   They are <u>above</u> the cheese.
2. Where are the apples?   They are <u>between</u> the eggs and the pineapple.
3. Where is the honey?   It is <u>next to</u> the jam.
4. Where is the pineapple? It is <u>below</u> the grapes. or   It is <u>next to</u> the apples.

Buying lunch, page 77

Conversation 1: 9
Conversation 2: 18

Words and sounds, page 78   l<u>i</u>ke   p<u>ie</u>   (l<u>i</u>st)   <u>ai</u>sle   b<u>uy</u>   b<u>i</u>ke

1. bowls, a blender, a lamp
2. It didn't work. It is broken.
3. She will go back to the shop today and talk to the shop assistant.
4. I'd like a new blender.

Words and sounds, page 79   c<u>oa</u>t   b<u>o</u>x   so   (g<u>o</u>)   n<u>o</u>

Unit 7 Going Places, page 80

1. by train   2. by bicycle   3. on foot
4. by plane   5. by taxi   6. by tram
7. by bus   8. by car   9. by motorbike   10. by boat

Places, page 81
1. Where do people post letters? Post Office
2. Where do people swim? swimming pool
3. Where do students study? school
4. Where do people put money? bank
5. Where do people watch movies? cinema
6. Where do people go to borrow books? library
7. Where do people go when they are sick? hospital
8. Where do people go to catch a train? train station
9. Where do people go to exercise? gym

Adam's story, page 81
1. When does Adam go to the library?   Thursday
2. How does he go there?   He walks there.
3. Where does Adam go on Friday?   He goes to the post office.
4. How does he go there?   He goes by bus.
5. When does Adam go to the cinema?   Every week
6. How does he go there?   He goes by car.

Write sentences about Adam, page 82

Every day Adam walks to the park with his dog.

He goes to the library on Thursday to borrow books.

Every week he goes by car to the cinema with his friend to watch a movie.

Train travel, page 82

a. ticket   b. timetable   c. platform
d. ticket office   e. ticket gate   f. ticket slot

Buying a train ticket, page 83

1. First, read the timetable for the train time and platform number.
2. 'Id like a return ticket to the city please.'
3. Put the ticket into the slot. Go through the gate and take the ticket.
4. Keep the ticket with him on the train.

Read the train timetable, page 83

What time will Joel arrive at Central? 10.44
How long will Joel be on the train?   29 minutes
What time is the next train from Westmead to Central? 11.15

page 84   1) First, read the timetable for the train time and the platform number.
2) Buy a ticket from the ticket office.
3) Go to the ticket gate and put the ticket into the slot.
4) Go through the gate and take the ticket with you.
5) Go to the platform and wait for the train.

Write the directions, page 85

It's in High Street.
Go along Main Street and turn right at High Street.

Boyer Educational Resources – Order Form (See our website for other order options)

NAME:_____ EMAIL:_____

ADDRESS:_____

CITY:_____ POSTCODE:_____ PHONE:_____ FAX:_____

Item	ISBN	Qty	RRP Aus$	
People in Australia's Past - their stories, their achievements	978 1 877074 34 9	☐	@ $12.95	_____
People in Australia's Past - Audio CD (narration of stories)	978 1 877074 35 6	☐	@ $19.95	_____
People in Australia's Past - language workbook (A4 Spiral)	978 1 877074 36 3	☐	@ $44.95	_____
Understanding Everyday Australian - Book One	978 0 9585395 0 0	☐	@ $29.95	_____
Understanding Everyday Australian - Audio CD One	978 1 877074 01 1	☐	@ $19.95	_____
Understanding Everyday Australian - Teacher's Book One	978 0 9585395 2 4	☐	@ $44.95	_____
Understanding Everyday Australian - Book One & Audio CD	978 1 877074 16 5	☐	@ $39.95	_____
Understanding Everyday Australian - Book Two	978 0 9585395 3 1	☐	@ $29.95	_____
Understanding Everyday Australian - Audio CD Two	978 1 877074 02 8	☐	@ $19.95	_____
Understanding Everyday Australian - Teacher's Book Two	978 0 9585395 5 5	☐	@ $44.95	_____
Understanding Everyday Australian - Book Two & Audio CD	978 1 877074 17 2	☐	@ $39.95	_____
Understanding Everyday Australian - Book Three	978 1 877074 20 2	☐	@ $29.95	_____
Understanding Everyday Australian - Audio CD Three	978 1 877074 21 9	☐	@ $19.95	_____
Understanding Everyday Australian - Teacher's Book Three	978 1 877074 22 6	☐	@ $44.95	_____
Understanding Everyday Australian - Book Three & Audio CD	978 1 877074 23 3	☐	@ $39.95	_____
Understanding Spoken English - Book One	978 1 877074 08 0	☐	@ $29.95	_____
Understanding Spoken English - Audio CD One	978 1 877074 10 3	☐	@ $19.95	_____
Understanding Spoken English - Teacher's Book One	978 1 877074 11 0	☐	@ $44.95	_____
Understanding Spoken English - Book One & Audio CD	978 1 877074 18 9	☐	@ $39.95	_____
Understanding Spoken English - Book Two	978 1 877074 12 7	☐	@ $29.95	_____
Understanding Spoken English - Audio CD Two	978 1 877074 14 1	☐	@ $19.95	_____
Understanding Spoken English - Teacher's Book Two	978 1 877074 15 8	☐	@ $44.95	_____
Understanding Spoken English - Book Two & Audio CD	978 1 877074 19 6	☐	@ $39.95	_____
Understanding Spoken English - Book Three	978 1 877074 24 0	☐	@ $29.95	_____
Understanding Spoken English - Audio CD Three	978 1 877074 25 7	☐	@ $19.95	_____
Understanding Spoken English - Teacher's Book Three	978 1 877074 26 4	☐	@ $44.95	_____
Understanding Spoken English - Book Three & Audio CD	978 1 877074 27 1	☐	@ $39.95	_____
Understanding English Pronunciation - Student book	978 0 9585395 7 9	☐	@ $29.95	_____
Understanding English Pronunciation - Audio CD (Set of 3)	978 1 877074 03 5	☐	@ $39.95	_____
Understanding English Pronunciation - Teacher's Book	978 0 9585395 9 3	☐	@ $44.95	_____
Spelling and Pronunciation for English Language Learners	978 1 877074 04 2	☐	@ $19.95	_____
Phonemic Charts of English Sounds A3 colour, laminated (set of 2)	978 1877074 05 5	☐	@ $16.95	_____
English Vowel Sound Spelling Charts A4 colour (20 reusable charts)	978 1877074 39 4	☐	@ $39.95	_____
Word Building Activities for Beginners of English	978 1 877074 28 8	☐	@ $29.95	_____
English Language Skills - Level 1 Student's Workbook	978 1 877074 29 5	☐	@ $19.95	_____
English Language Skills - Level 1 Audio CD	978 1 877074 31 8	☐	@ $19.95	_____
English Language Skills - Level 1 Teacher's Book	978 1 877074 32 5	☐	@ $49.95	_____
English Language Skills - Level 1 Teacher's Book & Audio CD	978 1 877074 33 2	☐	@ $59.95	_____

<u>Plus postage and handling within Australia</u>: **$8.50**

(Prices include GST & are correct at time of printing but may be subject to change.)   **Total Amount** _____

Method of payment: Cheque ___   MasterCard ___   Visa ___   Money Order ___

Credit Card Number: ☐☐☐☐ ☐☐☐☐ ☐☐☐☐ ☐☐☐☐   Card Expiry Date:_____

Card Holder's Name: _____ Card Holder's Signature: _____

Please make your cheque or money order payable to ***Boyer Educational Resources***

Fax your order to: **02 4739 1538**   (from outside Australia Ph/fax + 61 2 4739 1538)   Web address: **www.boyereducation.com.au**

Post your order to: **Boyer Educational Resources, PO Box 255, Glenbrook   NSW   2773**

Boyer Educational Resources books and audio CDs   www.boyereducation.com.au

'Understanding Everyday Australian' – series (books with audio CD)

NEW!
People in Australia's Past Reader (A5), Audio CD, Language workbook

'Understanding Spoken English' – (books with audio CD) international editions

Spelling and Pronunciation for English Language Learners	Understanding English Pronunciation	Word Building Activities for beginners of English	English Language Skills Level One

Spiral bound Teacher's Books with photocopiable activity pages, such as surveys, role cards & matching activities.

All our teacher's books are A4 size. Student's books contain language exercises and answers.